QUAKE III ARENA

Prima's Official Strategy Guide

Steve Honeywell

Prima Games
A Division of Prima
Communications, Inc.

3875 Atherton Road
Rocklin, CA 95765
(916) 632-4400
www.primagames.com

Project Editors: Richard Dal Porto and Michael Littlefield
Product Manager: Sara E. Wilson

ISBN: 7615-2588-2
Library of Congress Catalog Card Number: 99-67342
Printed in the United States of America

99 00 01 02 GG 10 9 8 7 6 5 4 3 2 1

contents

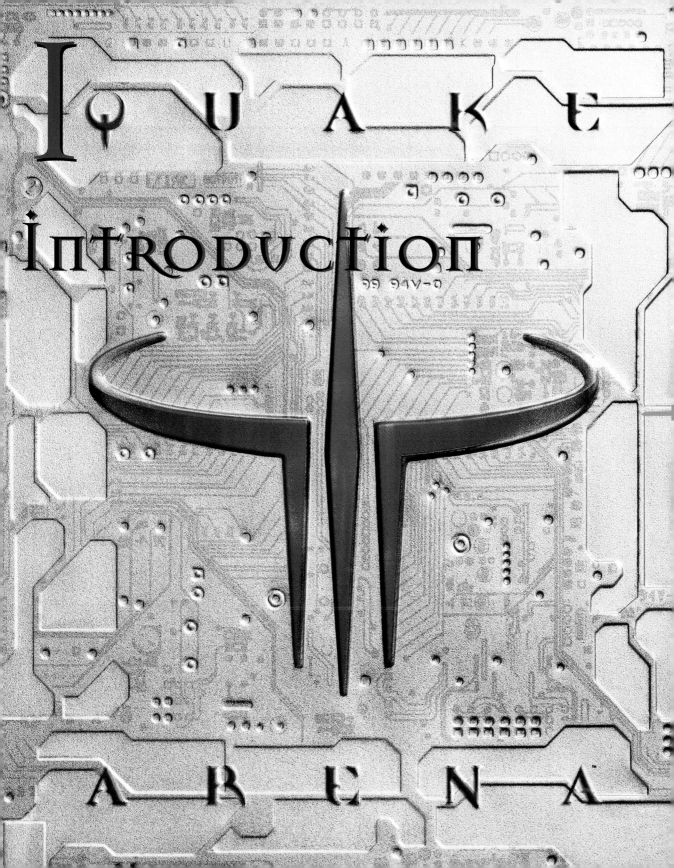

Quake

Introduction

Arena

THE ARENA ETERNAL

No one knows who they are or where they came from. All that is known is that a race of multidimensional creatures called the Vadrigar created the Arena Eternal for their own reasons.

The arenas exist to bring together the greatest warriors in the history of the universe. The Vadrigar select only the best fighters and place them in the arenas to fight, to kill, and to die. The battles are endless.

The Vadrigar have their reasons for these combats, and for tabulating the results. However, the reasons are not important. What is important is that now you are in the Arena Eternal. You fight, you die, and you rise to fight again. You must kill or be killed, and you will do both as you battle through the arenas.

How is Quake III Arena Different?

Players expecting *Quake III Arena* to be a repeat of the earlier versions of *Quake* are in for a big surprise. Unlike other first-person perspective games, *Quake III Arena* doesn't have the normal cast of enemy creatures. Instead, *Quake III Arena* is purely a game of deathmatches.

This fact makes even the single-player version of *Quake III Arena* very different from other games in the genre. For instance, there aren't dozens of enemies waiting for you on a given level. Instead, there's a handful of opponents moving through the level and searching for you.

Another significant difference is that, except in certain multiplayer games, it's every man for himself. The computer-generated enemies or other human players don't gang up on you—they're looking to kill each other as much as to kill you.

A major additional change is that *anyone* currently on a level can use any of the items there. You may be used to killing off monsters and then grabbing caches of health and ammunition. Now your enemies can run off with those items. Anything can be picked up by anyone.

There are other differences as well. Everything, from your recently killed enemies to the grenade launcher you just grabbed, respawns continually throughout the level. This is good for you in that items you need regenerate eventually. It's bad in that the same is true for all your enemies too.

How to Use this Book

There are a number of strategies that work on each of the maps. This book covers a number of possibilities for each map and shows you the important locations, both for finding items and for combat. Things to attack, how to defend yourself, good sniping positions—all of these are covered.

The one thing this book cannot do is play the game for you. Knowing where to find a railgun and a good sniping position doesn't make you invincible, or even viable. You must know how to use the railgun and be able to do it in combat, when split second reactions and pinpoint accuracy are critical. The red armor can't help you if you don't survive long enough to get it.

Think of this book as a travel guide. It can show you how to get to places, important things to see, and things to avoid. It can't teach you how to drive. If you want to improve your game, you must practice, both on your own and in combat against other human players. You'll take your lumps and pay your dues, but if you are dedicated, this book can point out the way to *Quake III Arena* dominance.

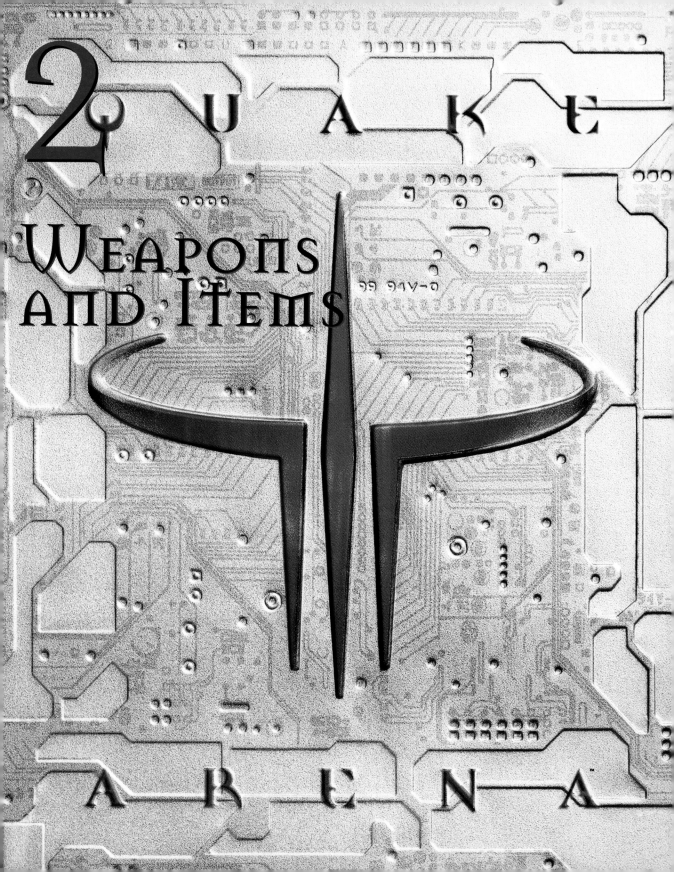

2uake

Weapons and Items

Arena

YOUR WEAPONS

GAUNTLET

The gauntlet should be used only in times of desperation.

The gauntlet is one of your default weapons. When you are completely out of ammunition for every other weapon, the only thing left is the gauntlet. Usable only at extremely close range, the buzz saw attached to the gauntlet does decent damage. However, it's almost impossible to use in the frenzied battles ahead. You should only use this weapon when absolutely necessary, and you should almost never get to that point. If you do frag someone with this weapon you recieve a humiliation award. And at the end of the level you recieve a medal.

The gauntlet is the most difficult weapon to use in combat, but its effects can be devastating.

Machine Gun

Your other default weapon is the machine gun, a much more useful tool than the gauntlet. What the machine gun lacks in raw power, it makes up in bullet availability and rate of fire. The machine gun is relatively accurate and can chew through enemy armor and health quickly. Whenever you start a level or respawn after dying, this is your available weapon. Always try to get a more powerful one quickly, but the machine gun is OK until you find something better.

The machine gun is a good choice until you find something better.

> ### Tip
>
> *While all other weapons (except the gauntlet) are better than the machine gun, it is good for strafing attacks because its rapid-fire capabilities allow you to deal out a lot of destruction very quickly.*

The machine gun uses bullets, which are common on most levels.

The machine gun doesn't do much damage, but with persistence, it can chew through the toughest enemies.

Shotgun

The next step up from the machine gun is the shotgun. Despite its slow rate of fire due to its considerable reload time, the shotgun offers a lot of bang for the buck. From a distance, the shotgun causes some damage, but at close range it can shatter an opponent with a single hit. On levels designed for close-quarters fighting, this is one of the best weapons in your arsenal. It's also great when you encounter enemies too busy with each other to notice you moving in for the kill.

The shotgun can kill virtually anyone at close range and does significant damage from a long distance.

Tip

Shotguns appear on virtually every level of Quake III Arena, so get used to using them. The shotgun is also your safest weapon because it can dish out tremendous damage without the negative splash damage of the rocket launcher or the BFG10K.

Boxes of shells are relatively common on levels that feature the shotgun.

The shotgun can cause incredible destruction up close.

Grenade Launcher

Perhaps your least predictable weapon is the grenade launcher. Unlike your other weapons, the projectiles fired from this one rattle around on the ground for a few seconds before they explode. Because of your enemies' speed, timing the grenade explosions is extremely difficult. Use the grenade launcher when you have the advantage of height, particularly above well-trafficked areas. Its biggest value is its potential for surprise.

Reckless use of grenades can often cause more damage to you than to your enemies.

Tip

The best place to use a grenade launcher is from above. That way, you avoid taking any splash damage from the explosions, and you can blanket a lower area with enough grenades to seriously damage everyone in the vicinity. Grenades explode on contact if they hit a foe before they bounce.

Grab the grenades to keep your grenade launcher effective.

Because it's difficult to use accurately, the grenade launcher is best used as a surprise weapon.

ROCKET LAUNCHER

The rocket launcher is one of your best friends in combat. It fires at an incredibly fast rate, and the rockets can shred any enemy with just a few hits. Even better, a near miss still causes damage from the explosion. Unfortunately, if you use this weapon at close range, you also take damage from the resulting explosion. At medium and long range, however, there's nothing much better than the rocket launcher.

One of the best weapons is found frequently.

Tip

Because the rocket launcher offers tremendous splash damage from the exploding rockets, you often cause more damage by aiming at the ground near enemies, rather than directly at them. Though a direct hit causes more damage, shooting the ground (or a wall directly behind your enemy) causes damage more consistently.

Since you often use the rocket launcher, boxes of rockets are a welcome sight.

A direct rocket hit usually leaves assorted pieces of the victim.

Rocket explosions can cause fatal damage even without a direct hit.

11

Lightning Gun

One of the new, exciting weapons in *Quake III Arena* is the lightning gun. This weapon discharges incredibly powerful bursts of pure electricity that can destroy any opponent. The lightning gun is less common than many of the other weapons, and ammunition is difficult to find. When you have the lightning gun, use it and don't horde the ammunition.

Its blasts of powerful electricity make this a weapon to be feared.

Tip

The lightning gun has a relatively short range; use it when things get up close and personal.

Boxes of ammo for the lightning gun are rare, they are especially prized.

A good range, rapid fire, and accuracy make the lightning gun a favorite weapon of many players.

Railgun

The railgun is one of the most powerful weapons available. The slugs it fires are extremely effective, ripping through the enemy and causing tremendous damage. They are also quite fast, which means you can hit with them accurately from a good distance. Unfortunately, the railgun cycles very slowly, so you only get a shot off every second or so. It's a tough weapon to use well, and it requires a lot of practice. Once you get the hang of it, though, it's a good find.

When it hits, the railgun can rip anyone apart.

Tip

No other Quake III Arena weapon requires as much practice as the railgun. To help your aim, use the zoom function to get a closer look at your target. Practice with this weapon whenever possible in the single-player game to get a feel for it. In the hands of a master, nothing is as deadly. Two railgun hits in a row earn an impressive medal.

Railgun ammo is rare.

It takes a steady hand and a quick trigger finger to kill with the railgun, but in the hands of an expert, nothing is more lethal.

Plasma Gun

Along with the machine gun and rocket launcher, one of the more reliable weapons is the plasma gun. It combines the rapid-fire capabilities of the machine gun with a whole lot more power and devastation capabilities. The plasma gun can rend an enemy with a few hits, and thanks to its great rate of fire, it can track speeding enemies down and rip them apart. Ammunition is somewhat common on levels with the plasma gun.

The plasma gun packs a huge wallop and has a tremendous rate of fire.

Tip

Think of the plasma gun as a more powerful version of the machine gun. Both offer a similar rate of fire, but the plasma gun has additional splash damage and much higher damage potential. Because this weapon does more damage than the machine gun, and because ammo tends to be less common, fire short bursts instead of continual streams of plasma charges.

Boxes of plasma cells keep you burning through enemies.

The plasma gun's power and high rate of fire make it a coveted weapon in Deathmatch. Beware, splash damage from the plasma gun can harm the shooter.

BFG10K

The heaviest hitter available is the BFG10K, a big freakin' gun that hits harder than anything else out there. Naturally, this is an incredibly rare weapon and is available only on a few levels. The BFG is almost always difficult to find, usually accessible only by locating secret areas. Ammunition is also rare. This weapon features a tremendous blast radius and is capable of killing virtually any enemy with a single hit.

The biggest, nastiest weapon in *Quake III Arena* is the BFG10K.

Tip

If you remember the BFG from earlier ID games, you may be surprised when you first use it in Quake III Arena. The new, improved BFG10K fires instantly instead of needing a few seconds to charge up. It still does incredible amounts of damage and features good splash damage potential, but the range of the splash damage is smaller. The BFG now also features an excellent rate of fire, and each shot uses only a single charge.

BFG ammo is rare, but when you see it, the granddaddy of weapons is somewhere nearby.

Note

Details on BFG jumping can be found in Chapter 3.

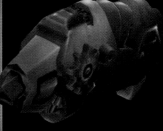

With the BFG, you can rain destruction on your enemies. It's only included on a few levels, so use it when it's available. Remember, splash damage may occur.

Armor items prevent some of the damage you take from enemy weapons. Gathering armor should be one of your priorities, ranking just behind finding a good, powerful weapon. Even though a full complement of armor won't stop you from being killed by a massive assault, it can deflect enough damage to keep you alive and fighting longer.

Note

It is possible to have over 100 points of armor. When you do, the points in excess of 100 slowly deteriorate, at the rate of about one point per second.

Armor shards are worth grabbing, but not worth going out of your way for.

Armor Shard

These small shards give you a few armor points. One isn't worth much, but you generally find shards in groups of four or five, which makes them well worth getting. Don't risk getting killed to grab armor shards, but try not to pass them up when you spot them.

Combat Armor

The yellow suits of armor are a welcome sight. When you grab one, it adds 50 points of armor to your total. These are relatively common and are worth getting whenever you spot them.

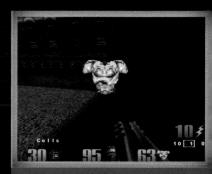

Combat armor gives you 50 points of armor instantly.

BODY ARMOR

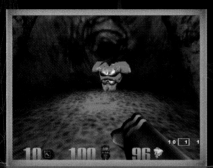

Red body armor is rare. Grabbing this is worth risking a frag.

Body armor is not very common in *Quake III Arena*, and with good reason. It instantly adds 100 armor points. When you spot body armor, go for it and be prepared to battle for it. It can keep you alive through a lot of enemy damage.

HEALTH ITEMS

When you are wounded, nothing looks better than a cache of health items. You can always be brought back to full health with a few of these items. Learn where they are, and go to them when you take damage.

Note

It is possible to have over 100 points of health. Like armor points, the points in excess of 100 slowly deteriorate, at the rate of about one point per second.

GREEN CROSS

Green crosses add only five health points, but they can take you over your maximum.

When you grab a green cross, you regain five points of health. In addition, green crosses generally appear in groups of four or five. Even better, these items can take you above your normal maximum of 100 health. Never pass them up.

Tip

Unless you are on the run from someone hot on your trail, always pick up any green crosses you see.

YELLOW CROSS

Yellow crosses are pretty common. Each one you grab gives back 25 health points—up to your normal maximum of 100.

Yellow crosses are worth 25 health points.

GOLD CROSS

Gold crosses are about half as common as yellow crosses. They are also twice as effective, adding 50 health points to your total—up to your normal maximum of 100.

A gold cross can take you from near dead to viable instantly.

POWER-UPS

On every level, there are several special items that appear in particular areas. These items give you special powers and abilities that can make you tougher, harder to hit, or much more powerful. These items are especially prized, so when you get one, exploit it. All of these power-ups last for about 30 seconds unless otherwise noted.

Note

If you are killed while using a special item, your enemies can get it from you. Guard special items carefully.

BATTLE SUIT

Battle suits are most frequently found on levels where lava or slime is common. When you grab a battle suit, you can ignore the effects of slime and lava and run through both without taking any damage. More importantly, this item also prevents you from taking splash damage from weapons, like rocket launchers, fired in your vicinity. When you have the battle suit a golden shield surrounds your body.

Battle suits don't appear too often, but they allow you to shrug off damage that would normally kill you.

Since you take no splash damage when using a battle suit, rocket and BFG jumps are painless.

Tip

You can travel in the more dangerous areas of a level with the battle suit. This allows you to attack enemies from angles and directions they may not expect.

Mega-Health

When you grab a Mega-Health, you instantly receive 100 health points. This is added to your total, regardless of what that total is. Therefore, if you snag it at full health, you have double the normal amount.

This blue icon is always a welcome sight, even when you are at full health.

Note

Unlike the other power-ups, the Mega-Health's effects last until you take damage. However, if the Mega-Health takes you above your 100 point maximum, those extra health points still slowly deteriorate.

Quad Damage

The Quad Damage icon does exactly what the name implies. It greatly multiplies the damage your weapon can cause. This is devastating with any weapon. When used with more powerful weapons like the rocket launcher or the lightning gun, you can kill even the most powerful enemy in a hot second.

The Quad is the most sought-after item in the game.

Tip

When you have the Quad, a glowing shell covers your body. Look for enemies with this effect on them and stay out of their way. Or, kill them and get the Quad for yourself.

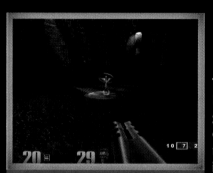

Regeneration works like a Mega-Health, but a little more slowly.

REGENERATION

The regeneration icon works similarly to the Mega-Health, but it adds health slowly over time. When you get this item, it tacks on five health points every second or so, and it can increase your health above the normal maximum of 100 points. While it doesn't have the instant effect of the Mega-Health, it can often add more points to your total over the long haul.

Note

When the regeneration icon wears off, you retain the health, but this slowly dissipates over time.

Take to the sky with the flight icon.

FLIGHT

The flight icon puts you above your enemies in a real way. The effects of this icon last for about 30 seconds, and from the air you can hit your enemies from positions that make it very difficult for them to retaliate. Flight is only available in multiplayer games.

Tip

When you start to hear the flight icon wearing off, head for the ground or suffer the effects of a potentially long fall.

Haste

One of the best ways to protect yourself is to keep moving and use your speed to make yourself more difficult to hit. The haste icon doubles your speed, which makes you an even tougher target than normal.

Blinding speed makes you difficult to hit.

Invisibility

Invisibility icons aren't too common. When you get one, you're shrouded and nearly impossible to see—you look like a shimmering haze. Enemies can still spot you but are less likely to do so. Therefore, they have a much tougher time hitting you.

They can't kill what they can't see. Get this icon to attack from the shadows.

Enemies using invisibility are hard to see and harder to kill.

Tip

Standing still negates the usefulness of invisibility. When you have it, keep moving and keep your enemies guessing.

The personal teleporter acts like the teleportation portals you find in many of the arenas, with a few differences. First, it can be used whenever and wherever you want. Second, it teleports you randomly to a respawn point on the level. If you are in trouble, you can use this item to get out of danger, but the teleporter might pull you out of one tough situation and drop you into another one. This item remains in your inventory until you use it.

The personal teleporter is an insurance policy that can sometimes pay dividends.

Tip

On levels that have Fog of Death or a Void, keep the personal teleporter in case you fall off the side. Often, this is the only way to save yourself.

The medkit acts like a Mega-Health, but you can use it whenever you wish.

Medkit

The medkit syringe, like the personal teleporter, remains in your inventory until you use it. When you trigger it, you immediately return to full health. It's a great insurance policy, but make sure you get out of harm's way after using it, or you'll only delay the inevitable.

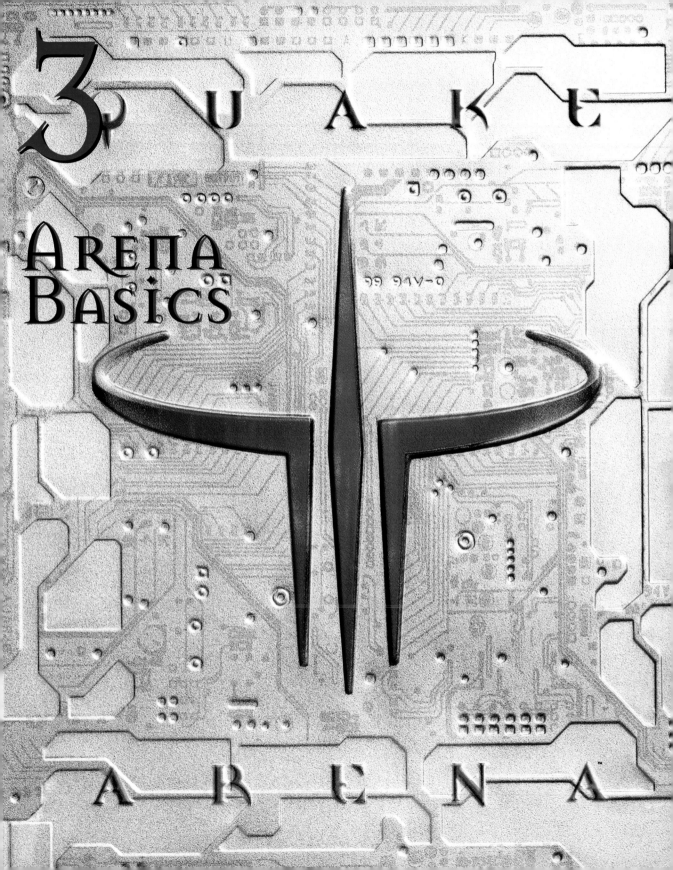

3 QUAKE

Arena Basics

ARENA

Configuring Your Game

The single most important set of decisions you make in *Quake III Arena* is determining the configuration of your controls. How you control yourself in the game can make the difference between playing well and getting fragged.

There is no one right way to configure the controls. Talk to 100 *Quake* players, and you will get 100 different configurations. The most important thing is to make sure that it works for you. The basic idea is to get all of your most important commands in the same area of the keyboard so you can access them easily. You don't want to have to hunt for the right key to jump or use your personal teleporter in the middle of a firefight, because that's what gets you killed.

In addition to keeping the keys accessible to you, make your configuration comfortable to use. Design your configuration in a way that makes sense to you. If the mouse button in other games you've played fires a weapon, use it the same way in *Quake III Arena*. If you are comfortable using the cursor keys for movement, configure them the same way here.

Don't ever give up the mouse. Using the mouse is the fastest way to look around the environment. A mouse button configured to shoot gives you a very natural combination of looking and firing at a particular target, almost like pointing and clicking on your desktop.

Similarly, you may want to set the Always Run option on. In most cases, running is the preferred method of travel since it allows you to cover ground faster. This gives you more speed to pursue enemies and get away from them. The instances when you do want to slow to a walk are rare.

Note

Running, while considerably faster than walking, is also considerably noisier. The largest benefit to walking is that it is silent.

The game automatically saves your control selections to a configuration file that is stored in your Quake III Arena folder. Switching your key configuration when you start playing isn't much trouble, but changing it once you have gotten used to another forces you to suffer a long relearning process. Once you are happy with a particular configuration, make changes only when absolutely necessary.

Movement Basics

In *Quake III Arena*, shooting accuracy is incredibly important, as is knowledge of the arenas. However, the most important thing is knowing *how* to move. Mobility, along with accuracy and knowledge, is key to *Quake III* Arena success. It seems so basic that it's easy to forget.

Walking and Running

In general, you should keep moving in any of the arenas. Standing still does make it easier to aim, but it creates a number of significant problems. First, when you aren't moving you are a sitting duck for anyone who wanders into the area. There's nothing that a good *Quake III* Arena player (or one of the computer-controlled characters) likes to see more than an enemy standing still. This is the biggest drawback to staying in one place.

There are a few other problems associated with not moving. One is that you tend to encounter fewer enemies, which means fewer opportunities to score frags. A player standing still might see one or two opponents run past, but a player actively running through the arena might have half a dozen encounters or more.

It doesn't sound like learning to move is difficult, but there are many tricks you can learn to both attack and defend more effectively.

Don't let your enemies catch you flat-footed.

The other problem is that by standing still, you don't run across any new items. If you never move from a particular location, you never get more powerful. You must keep moving if you want to improve your stock of weapons, heal, and gain armor.

Standing still will get you pegged. If you keep moving, you are harder to hit.

Jumping

Much of your strategy in *Quake III Arena* is naturally focused around avoiding damage. Jumping is one of the best ways to keep yourself from getting fragged.

Normal Jumps

Jumping certainly can help you move from place to place more quickly. Jumps over low walls, down stairs, or up stairs help you move across a map much more rapidly. Even hopping on flat ground makes you move forward more briskly.

By moving constantly, you can improve your variety of weapons and increase your armor.

Tip

Practice, practice, practice. Getting used to jumping constantly is difficult, but it is one of the most important basic strategies to improving your game.

The other reason for jumping is that it helps you avoid splash damage from some weapons. Many players, especially other human players, aim weapons like rocket launchers and the BFG10K at the ground near you instead of directly at you. Their hope is that rather than being hit with the weapon, you'll be damaged and killed by the impact of the weapon against the floor or the ground.

Jumping around helps you avoid this sort of damage. By keeping yourself in the air as much as possible, you avoid much of the splash damage that would have affected you if you were still on the ground. The additional speed you have with the jumping also helps you close the distance between you and your enemies, forcing them to change weapons or risk blowing themselves up.

Bounce Pads and Acceleration Pads

Bounce pads appear both on the ground and on angles on many of the maps. Running into or over a bounce pad sends you into the air. Each bounce pad has a particular trajectory; some send you directly into the air while others send you sailing off at angles.

Where running along the ground gets you hit, jumping helps you avoid damage. Many of your foes jump constantly.

Both flat and angled bounce pads send you sailing into the sky.

! Caution

Bounce pads not only have a set trajectory, but the nature of your jump causes you to pause at the apex of the bounce. You are a sitting duck for a skilled railgun user, and you are open to being nailed with a number of other weapons as well.

Tip

If you don't want to use a bounce pad set in the floor, you can jump over it.

Acceleration pads look like ramps to nowhere. Stepping onto an acceleration pad launches you across the map to a location on the other side. You often find acceleration pad leaps over deadly terrain. Usually, these jumps take you to a particularly powerful weapon or power-up.

Rocket Jumps and BFG10K Jumps

Two important techniques to learn and perfect are the rocket jump and the BFG jump. In addition to being useful as weapons, both of these items can help you reach hard-to-find sniping positions.

Acceleration pads launch you over canyons toward important objects.

There is a trick to executing a rocket jump and taking as little damage as possible. To perform this maneuver, point your rocket launcher at the ground, then jump. As soon as you jump, fire the rocket launcher straight into the floor. The force of the explosion sends you flying into the air dozens of feet higher than a normal jump.

A rocket jump allows you to get much higher above the ground.

While you can rocket jump by leaping and firing the weapon simultaneously, you take a tremendous amount of splash damage from the rocket. Always jump first to avoid the damage.

Rocket jumping can be used to find some good sniping locations. It can also be used to facilitate moving through a map much more quickly. In general, you can rocket jump up about 15-20 virtual feet. This allows you to go up from a lower floor to a higher one without the need for a staircase or ramp.

Some great sniping locations are only reachable by rocket jumping.

Tip

You can often find health items immediately after rocket jumping up to a higher floor. This negates the health losses from the jump, making it a very worthwhile effort to move from place to place this way.

Tip

You take no splash damage from rocket jumping if you are wearing the battle suit.

Rocket jump off a bounce pad to go even higher.

For an even higher jump, rocket jump off a bounce pad. The trick here is to fire the rocket launcher directly into the center of the pad just after you bounce off of it. This sends you up to locations much higher than you could reach normally. Some areas are inaccessible except by rocket jumping off a bounce pad.

You can also increase the height of your jump with the BFG10K. To perform a BFG jump, simply use the BFG in place of the rocket launcher. This takes you much higher than the rocket launcher, but you also take more damage.

! Caution

Be very cautious when rocket or BFG jumping while you have the Quad. You must be at virtually perfect health and be nearly flawless in your technique just to survive.

Take care when jumping with the BFG10K.

Air Control

Since jumping is so critical to your success, it follows that learning to control yourself while in the air is equally important. Some maps rely heavily on acceleration pads and bounce pads. However, against good players, your trajectory off these pads is known and leaves you wide open to a railgun shot. The solution to this problem, as well as a way to help you land where you want to go, is air control.

Air control works exactly the same way as movement on the ground. If you want your jump to carry you forward, hold down your forward movement key. If you don't want to cover as much distance, pull back. You can also move to the left and right and turn in either direction when you are in the air.

Air control is perhaps the single most important aspect of movement to practice—next to rocket jumping. In fact, proper control of yourself in the air is critical to rocket jumping and BFG jumping accurately. Work on changing your direction off bounce pads and acceleration pads so that you can use them with less chance of being nailed by a good player.

While your trajectory is set from an acceleration pad, you can easily alter where you land with air control, as shown in the second picture.

Shooting Basics

Movement is all well and good, but you won't score any frags unless you actually start firing your weapon. Learning how and when to fire—as well as what to fire—will help you score the necessary number of frags to pass any arena.

Strafing

New players tend to attack *Quake III Arena* in a very linear way, moving straight ahead or straight backwards. When these new players spot an enemy, they run right for them, and when the battle turns sour, they retreat in a straight line away. Both of these techniques will get you killed by a good, or even average, player. The most important fighting technique to learn is strafing.

Practice turning and firing in mid-jump or midbounce as well.

Side-to-Side Strafing

The simplest method of strafing is simply moving side-to-side. While firing in one direction, hold either the right or left movement key, your sidestep keys. This causes you to step out of the way of any incoming fire that was aimed at your previous location. You can bob from side-to-side while firing to become a much more difficult target.

Running in a straight line makes for an easy frag for your opponents.

The idea behind the strafe is that you can keep your weapon centered on your target while moving out of the way. Turning and running prevents you from retaliating against any enemy that isn't directly in front of you. By sidestepping or strafing, you can continue to fire back at your enemy.

A simple sidestep prevents a lot of potential pain.

While you can strafe and sidestep in open terrain, it is much more useful to do so when there is cover. Small alcoves in hallways, pillars, statues, and other aspects of the arenas provide some protection from enemy attacks. You can pop out, take a shot or two, then duck back into cover where your enemy can't see you. Statues and pillars have the added benefit of getting in the way of rockets, BFG shots, and plasma, meaning that you can also avoid a lot of splash damage this way.

Tip

To make yourself even harder to hit, try jumping and strafing at the same time. Getting used to moving in one direction, jumping, and firing a weapon all at the same time takes a lot of practice, but doing so pays dividends.

Circle Strafing

A step up from the simple sidestep is strafing in a circular pattern. Here, you not only move to the side as you fire, but you change the direction you are pointing, forming a roughly circular pattern. Doing this, and keeping your view centered on your target, allows you to deal continual damage on an enemy while presenting a much harder target to hit.

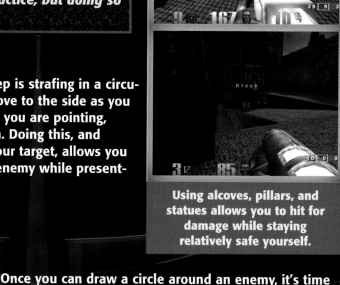

Using alcoves, pillars, and statues allows you to hit for damage while staying relatively safe yourself.

Moving in a circular pattern makes you harder to hit.

Once you can draw a circle around an enemy, it's time to include the forward and backward movement keys in your strafing. Now, instead of simply moving from side-to-side or in a circle, you can either approach or retreat from an opponent while continually changing the direction you are moving.

The most important thing in strafing and circle strafing is to learn to be unpredictable. If you always strafe to the left, your opponents (especially human ones) will figure this out and expect it. Learn to strafe in a relatively random pattern to avoid falling into a rut.

Tip

Mix random strafing with moving forwards and backwards and jumping, and you will present your enemies with a very difficult target to hit.

Sniping

There are times when you want to take a short break from running around a level and wait for an enemy. Setting up an ambush is something of a challenge. While you often get the jump on an enemy, you can find yourself sitting flat-footed when a powerful opponent runs in and starts firing.

Still, there are cases when sniping can pick up a few good kills. Whether you find a particularly deadly spot thanks to a good rocket jump, or locate a darkened corner with a good view of a desirable item, camping out and waiting can sometimes pay off.

Don't always move in the same direction.

There are two important aspects to sniping effectively. The first is to find a good sniping location. The perfect sniping spot is high up, shrouded in shadows, offers a good view of the arena, and is protected from at least two sides. The high vantage point allows you to rain death down on your enemies while remaining a more difficult target. Shadows naturally make you harder to see, which adds to the element of surprise when you hit an enemy from seemingly nowhere.

If you love camping, a good sniping spot is your best friend.

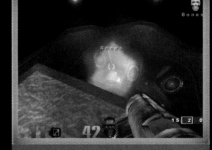

There are drawbacks to even the best sniper spot.

You want to have a good view of a large area from a sniper's post, or at least a clear view of an item that all of the other players want—the rocket launcher, the Quad, or what have you. Sniping over a shotgun doesn't usually pay the same sort of dividends as sniping over a more powerful weapon. Having a large area simply presents you with more targets.

The other requirement of a good sniping post is that it should be at least partially protected. Since you are concentrating your view on a particular location, you are open to having someone come up behind you and frag you with your back turned. The best sniping posts are accessible only by rocket jumps, which keeps other players from shooting you in the back.

Make sure what you are guarding is worthwhile.

While this sniping post is high and offers a clear view of the level below, it is accessible from three sides. Don't stay here too long.

The other important element to sniping is finding the right weapon. Without question, the railgun is the ultimate sniper's weapon. It requires precision, which is easier to accomplish from a position where you aren't moving and shooting at the same time. Additionally, the railgun projectile is an instantaneous hit from across the map. Firing at an enemy hundreds of virtual feet away with the railgun hits instantly, while other weapons take several seconds to get where they are going.

The railgun is the weapon of choice for snipers.

Because of its splash radius, the BFG also makes a good sniping weapon. In spite of its much slower shots, you can snipe quite effectively with the rocket launcher if you are patient and can lead your targets.

You can also snipe effectively with the BFG or rocket launcher.

Tip

Because of the nature of the weapon, the grenade launcher can also be an effective sniping tool. While it is generally less accurate than other weapons, its ability to completely blanket an area with explosions should not be underrated.

TERRAIN BASICS

Terrain plays a major part as you move through the arenas of *Quake III Arena*. The ground you walk on comes in a number of important varieties. Some terrain is equipped with gaps that allow you to fire at enemies through the floor. Other terrain is noisier when you walk on it. Some terrain is deadly or even fatal if you walk across it. You must keep aware of the terrain in the area. Knowing its characteristics can literally save your life.

Normal Terrain

Most of the terrain in *Quake III Arena* is safe to walk on. With few exceptions, your speed over normal, flat terrain is standard whether you are running on stone, concrete, or metal. There are some differences in these terrain types, but not in terms of your ability to get across them.

Floors

Level ground is the rule rather than the exception in the Arena Eternal. While some levels look to be made up of nothing but endless staircases, the fact is that flat terrain is by far the most common element of all of the arenas. Naturally, you spend most of your time on these areas.

There is no significant difference between the floor types when it comes to movement. You're just as fast and just as able to jump when running on a stone floor as you are on a metal floor. In terms of practicing or fighting, anything you can do on one type of flooring, you can do on another.

> ## Tip
> *The main difference between terrain types is simply the sound you make when running across them. As you might expect, moving along a metal floor is much louder than running on other types of material.*

While your speed is the same regardless of the flooring, the sound you make changes from surface to surface.

Bridges

Bridges are common in the game. In most respects, bridges are no different from standard floors, except that there are no walls to your sides. This has both benefits and problems. The biggest problem with being on a bridge or catwalk is that it's easy to fall off the side. For bridges suspended over normal terrain, this isn't much of a problem. However, many of the bridges in *Quake III Arena* run over slime, lava, and the red fog of death, where falling in is even more harmful to your score than taking a Quad-powered rocket to the face.

The benefit to bridges is huge. Most (though by no means all) of the bridges you encounter are above the surrounding terrain, or at least on the same level with the rest of the terrain. The lack of walls makes it very difficult for your enemies to damage you with splash-effect weapons, like rocket launchers and plasma guns, since there is no wall behind you for them to target.

Strafe with care when on bridges over deadly terrain.

You present a tougher target when up high.

Stairs and Ramps

Stair and ramp areas are much like normal floors and bridges in terms of the material of their construction. Your movement across them is considerably different though. Stairs and ramps slow you down to some extent to reflect the added effort required in climbing them. You are almost always a little less mobile in these areas than you are on flat terrain.

Dangerous Terrain

There are many ways to get hurt or killed by the terrain. Some of these are a function of the terrain itself, and one way simply depends on how you interact with the terrain. We'll discuss this first.

Stairs and ramps can slow your movement down.

Note

Any time you are killed by terrain, you have a frag taken away from you.

Falling

You can fall about the equivalent of a single story, or a level, without ill effects. Longer falls strip away some of your health. Generally speaking, even the longest fall only takes away about 10 points of health, and most long falls only strip a point or two from your total. In general, you don't need to worry about falls unless you are badly wounded. Still, fall enough times and you can end up in a body bag.

Lava and Slime

Slime is green while lava is red. Any time you walk through or fall into slime or lava, you start losing health immediately and rapidly. However, lava does more damage than slime. The battle suit is the only way to travel in lava or slime safely.

Short falls don't hurt you, but a long drop takes off some health.

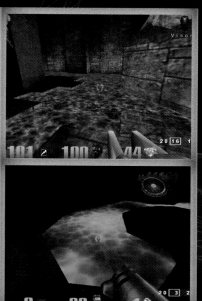

You can survive a swim in lava and slime, but you won't be happy with your health total.

Tip

When you fall into lava or slime, start jumping immediately. Move as quickly as possible to solid ground. While you'll be badly damaged and easily killed by the next person to see you, at least you won't have a frag taken away.

THE FOG OF DEATH

Many levels have low areas shrouded in a yellowish fog, which is harmless, although it clouds your vision. The red fog is quite different, however. The red fog of death only appears in low regions below the main area of the level. It is common on higher-tier levels around bridges and open platforms. If you fall into the fog of death, you die as soon as you hit the ground. There is no way out unless you are equipped with the personal teleporter and are incredibly fast with activating it. Since most of the fog of death pits are very shallow, this is unlikely.

Dying from the fog is a painful way to go.

Tip

While the fog of death is fatal if you fall in, don't be afraid to jump over it. You often have more than enough jumping ability to clear the fog, and this is sometimes the fastest way to move from place to place.

OUTER SPACE

On the highest tiers in the Arena Eternal, the maps occur in outer space. A fall into outer space off the side of an arena is another sure way to die. This is similar in many ways to the fog of death, but the falls here tend to be quite a bit longer. If you've got the personal teleporter, you have an excellent chance to use it before you are killed by the fall.

The drop is long, which just prolongs the pain.

Tip

On the highest-tier arenas, be extremely careful around the edges of the maps. These maps feature only small lips around the edges, not high walls, so if you aren't careful, you can run off the map quite easily.

Drowning

Several of the arenas contain pools of water that you can swim in. Generally, you should do at least a little swimming because these pools usually contain valuable items. However, you can only hold your breath for so long. After a little time spent underwater, you must surface to catch your breath. Like falling damage, the initial stages of drowning don't take away too much from your health total. However, once you start taking damage, head to the surface as quickly as you can. If you are at full health, you should have little problem exploring any body of water with time to spare.

Don't stay underwater for too long.

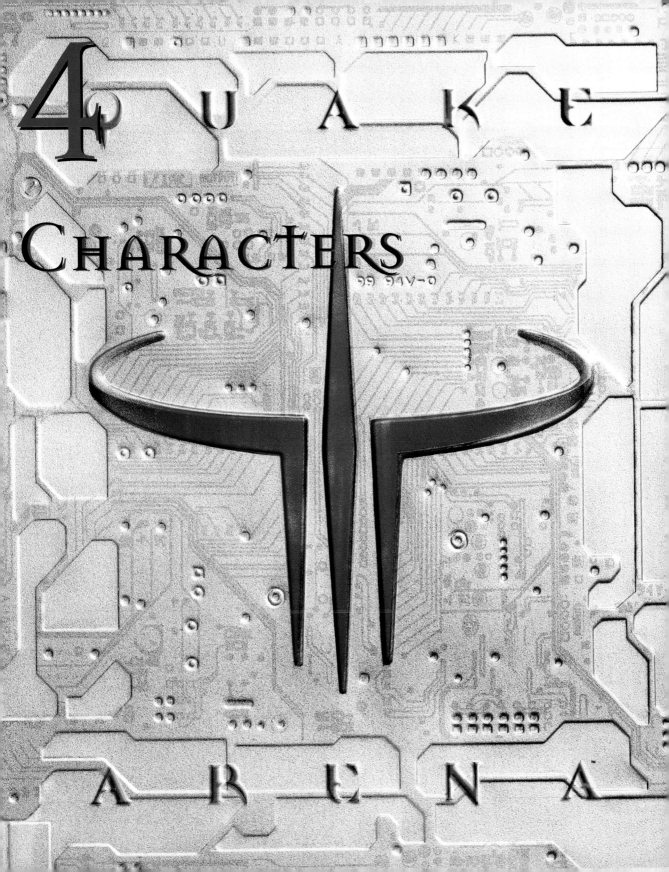

Unlike the previous *Quake* games, *Quake III Arena* contains no "monsters." Instead, you fight against characters using the same weapons and who are subject to the same problems as you. In each arena, you face off against at least one and as many as five or six enemies, each capable of pulping you with a well-fired rocket, or being crushed with a burst of plasma. Learn their tricks and weaknesses well because that may be the only thing that saves you.

Note

You create your own character at the start of a game. Pick the one you like best because all are identical when it comes to actual gameplay. All of the characters, when played by you, move at the same speed and can take the same amount of damage.

THE TRAINING LEVEL AND FIRST TIER ENEMIES

CRASH

Long ago, Crash was Doom's instructor and helped turn him into a one-man killing machine. Now, Crash's function is to act as the trainer for all new combatants in the Arena Eternal. For the most part, she keeps her temper and offers sound advice for the trials to come. However, she occasionally expresses some anger at particularly slow students.

RANGER

Ranger has paid the ultimate sacrifice for his world. Trained to protect the Earth at all costs and dedicated to no other task, Ranger was sent through slipgate after slipgate, from world to world, and from battle to battle. He survived, partly by luck and mostly from skill. After so many battles, there is little of the original man left. Even his real name is gone. He knows his world is safe, but he also knows there is no way back home. He is resigned to his fate in the Arena Eternal, and while it's not what he would have chosen for himself, he knows that this is his destiny, and he is determined to survive.

Ranger loves both the rocket launcher and the plasma gun. He tends to go for the rocket launcher more often, but he's just as likely to use either if he's got them both. When it's available to him, he also likes to go for a railgun. Ranger is much more likely to throw an insult your way, and even if you peg him with a good shot, most of his praise is of the back-handed sort.

PHOBOS

One of the original combatants in the Arena Eternal, Captain Eldon "Phobos" Brock has been fighting for a long time. This marine led the return of troops to the demon-plagued Mars base, where his mission was to destroy any last vestiges of the demon infestation. Unfortunately, Phobos learned all too quickly that the rest of his team had other orders. His new mission is to survive in the Arena Eternal, which means he'll be doing his best to kill you and anyone else who gets in his way.

Phobos loves the rocket launcher, and he's also prone to go for a railgun when there's one in the area. He also prefers getting a haste icon above almost any other item, when one becomes available. Phobos is more than a little paranoid, and this tends to show up in his comments during the battle.

Mynx

Smart, sexy, and dangerous, Mynx is something of a quandary. Some know her from her time on the fashion runway; others know her from her adult film roles. A select few know that Mynx was one of the world's top assassins—no job too tough, no job too small, no fee too large.

Mynx adores the shotgun and never hesitates to use it. However, her first real love in terms of weaponry is the grenade launcher, which she uses in preference of anything else. She tends to run constantly, camping out at a particular location only rarely. She also doesn't usually hold a grudge when killed frequently by one player. Mynx's commentary tends to be a little racier than most of the characters.

Orbb

The oddest-looking creature in the Arena Eternal is Orbb, a mechanical construct. Orbb was originally created by the Arena Masters to watch and record the battles. It soon became tired of simply viewing the combats and took up weapons to join in the fight. The second most disturbing thing about Orbb is its appearance—a gigantic eyeball mounted on the human-like arms it uses for mobility. The *most* disturbing thing about Orbb is its ability to slaughter anything in its way.

Orbb is relatively comfortable with any weapon but has a preference for the plasma gun. It also has a distinct fondness for the Quad and stops at almost nothing to grab it. On levels with Orbb and the Quad, you can often see Orbb lurking nearby, waiting for the Quad to appear. Orbb's comments tend merely to be disjointed attempts at conversation.

SARGE

Sarge has spent his entire adult life in combat. Sarge rightfully claims to be a master of modern warfare, and he's used virtually every weapon made anywhere at one time or another. Half killing machine, half drill sergeant, Sarge is the quintessential enlisted man, never complaining, but doing his job and plugging ahead.

Sarge is extremely aggressive, always moving to attack regardless of the personal cost. He retreats only rarely. He's also a much better shot than the other enemies up to this point. Sarge is quite competent with the rocket launcher and prefers it to any other weapon. He also goes after the Quad or a regeneration icon over any other power-up. Sarge's praise doesn't happen often, so take what you can get.

THE SECOND TIER ENEMIES

HOSSMAN

Hossman is deceptive. He looks slow, stupid, and clumsy, but he is none of these things. Hossman is quite fast for his size, extremely agile, and brighter than average. And that's just the beginning. As a former professional bodyguard, Hossman learned early that staying aware was the key to surviving. He's got the skills to keep a client alive, or to bump the client off if the situation seems right for it.

Hossman falls about in the middle in terms of his overall aggression and tendency to hold a grudge. He has a love for the lightning gun and likes the rocket launcher too. His comments tend to be pretty direct. If he doesn't respect you, you'll know it.

Daemia

The life of a bounty hunter is never an easy one; do it long enough and you'll see just about everything eventually. Daemia Maria Ruiz will kill anything for the right price, and over the course of her career, she's killed about everything that walks, talks, or crawls. By now, she's seen things that would give even the toughest career campaigner nightmares, but Daemia shrugs them off and blows them away.

Daemia is a very good shot, and she's a tough target because of her penchant for jumping. Daemia's first love in terms of weapons is the shotgun, although she never hesitates to grab the rocket launcher when it is available. She's not shy about using the grenade launcher either. Daemia also loves the Quad, and will seek it out. Daemia takes her skills seriously and doesn't much fancy your chances, even when you kill her.

Bitterman

What happens to a war hero badly mutated in the service of humanity? If that hero is Bitterman, he buries the past as deep as he can. On Stroggos, Bitterman released a demon inside himself and rained destruction on the Stroggs. There, Bitterman's demon within brought revenge and retribution. On Earth, it would bring pain and horror. In the Arena Eternal, it brings victory.

Bitterman is a decent shot, no more or less aggressive than the average. He loves the shotgun, as well as the Quad, which he seeks out constantly. His comments betray his southern roots, and even in combat and his mutated state, Bitterman retains some aspects of a true southern gentleman.

Grunt

Those lousy Stroggs. Sure, they were the enemy, but there was no reason for them to kill off the rest of Grunt's fire team like that. Even that worthless lieutenant didn't deserve to die that way. Now it's time for all the Stroggs to pay. Unfortunately for everyone else in the area, Grunt can no longer tell Strogg foes from the rest of the world. Grunt is ready to kill anything that stands in his way, and at this point, he thinks anything moving is standing in his way.

Despite his desire to kill anything in his path, Grunt is more likely than most to seek out methods to keep himself healthy. He's a wizard with the railgun and loves using it more than anything else. However, he'll happily settle for a rocket launcher. His comments tend to be short and to the point.

Hunter

When the Sorg Clan arrived on Tau Ceti, the colonies there were ravaged to supply body parts to the Cyborgers. Few of the original colonists survived. Hunter is one of those colonists. She has sacrificed her name, her past, and her future to become an instrument of vengeance for her people. Her goal is the complete destruction of the Sorg Clan. Until the last of the Sorg are killed, Hunter will know no peace. Her quest for revenge has been expanded to include any who stand in her way of destroying the Sorg.

Hunter is well attuned to the weapons that appear in her arena. She has a special fondness for, and deadly skill with, the lightning gun. She also frequently refers to herself as "we."

The Third Tier Enemies

Gorre

The clones of Visor (see the "Visor" section) are many in the Arena Eternal, but few have risen to the level of Gorre. According to Gorre, no one is better than he is in the arenas, but there's a reason he's in the third tier instead of a higher one. He's certainly capable of giving you a serious challenge, but don't let his constant bragging throw you off. If he were as good as he thinks, he'd be challenging Xaero for dominance.

In many ways, Gorre is the quintessential fighter. He has no major preferences, other than a slight penchant for the railgun and the rocket launcher. He also doesn't actively seek out particular power-ups and doesn't camp more or less than average. Most of his commentary is about his favorite subject, himself, and unfavorable comparisons of you to him.

Wrack

Wrack has memories...somewhere. There's not a lot left from his former life, and what there is comes in bursts and flashes. He can recall training for...something, and there are some memories of fighting large and nasty creatures. He can remember other arenas at times, although not these arenas, and the ones he remembers, like anything from the good ol' days, were better. The explosions were louder and the rockets were bigger. Most importantly, he was better. He brags that he was the master of the arenas once, but things aren't like they used to be.

Wrack is unusual in that he jumps less than average for a third-tier enemy. He loves the plasma gun and uses it more than any other weapon. Wrack's comments drift in and out of coherence. Sometimes he knows what's going on; other times, he seems to be having flashbacks to an earlier time (or an earlier game).

SLASH

Slash has almost limitless street cred, thanks to her years of blading for the L.A.-based branch of the Yakuza. When given a courier job, no one was faster, and no one was more capable of blasting her way through obstacles. Slash has enhanced herself liberally with cybronic implants and may now be more machine than human. Unlike the other combatants, Slash moves on force skates that keep her a few inches above the ground at all times. While the skates do make her a little taller, they also make her a lot faster and more agile.

The two things Slash craves more than anything are the BFG10K and the Quad, a combination that can give her a tremendous lead in any arena. Her comments to you belie the fact that Slash definitely knows what she is doing.

ANGEL

When cybronics started to become the norm, it was only a matter of time before someone tried to construct the perfect companion. The name of Angel's creator is lost to history, but unfortunately, Angel is still around. She turned on her creator and killed him before she was finished. Parts are still missing from Angel, including such niceties as compassion and mercy. What isn't missing is her lust for battle and her desire to kill anything she sees.

Angel prefers the rocket launcher, although she is equally at home with the railgun. She generally doesn't go too far out of her way for any of the power-ups. Angel is convinced of the superiority of her technological origin and won't hesitate to tell you about it too.

Klesk

Chitinids like Klesk are part of a larger consciousness, a hive mind. The constant chattering and noise becomes a comfortable environment. For Klesk, the chatter is gone. It no longer knows the hive mind. Instead, new voices have arisen, telling it that it must destroy the minds that churn around it constantly. When it quells these, Klesk will again know peace and will become the first of a new and proud race of Chitinids. It fights not only for its own sanity, but for the future of its own kind.

Klesk is both incredibly aggressive when it has the upper hand and likely to break off combat if it is going poorly. Klesk prefers the railgun which he is quite deadly with but likes to use the plasma gun as well. Its speeches show its alien origin and its dependence on the voices in its head.

The Fourth Tier Enemies

TankJr

The Tank Commander of Stroggos carved out a huge empire before being destroyed. That empire was the birthright of TankJr, reputedly the son of the Tank Commander and an Iron Maiden of Stroggos. Still young and curious about the ways of the universe, TankJr is consumed by hatred of his opponents and any who would stand in the way of his reclaiming his "right" to begin his father's empire anew. His background makes him virtually unable to communicate except through the language of destruction.

TankJr is incredibly vengeful and pursues an opponent with complete disregard for his own personal safety. If he can get the rocket launcher, he will, and the only thing TankJr loves more than a rocket launcher is the Quad. TankJr is completely mechanical, even more so than Angel, and his attempts at conversation reveal this.

LUCY

Earlier in her life, Lucy was a prison guard, keeping the inmates in line. During a massive prison break, Lucy did her best to keep the prisoners in line, permanently. When the riots were over, the powers-that-be decided that Lucy had spent too much time on one side of the bars and really belonged on the other side. When the system went down again, Lucy went back to the guns, and this time, she didn't wait around to see what the higher-ups would do with her.

There's only one thing that Lucy treasures more than the Quad, and that's a rocket launcher. She goes to extreme lengths to get her hands on a rocket launcher and is usually in the vicinity of where one appears on a given level. Lucy is convinced of her own femininity and dares anyone to see differently.

BIKER

The boss told Biker and his gang that they had to battle the Stroggs. Biker didn't see much sense in that—no money in busting Strogg heads. So he and his gang went back to riding their bikes and breaking kneecaps. Not the sharpest knife in the drawer, Biker is plenty tough and hostile to make up for it. More at home in a bar fight with a sawed-off pool cue in his hands, Biker has adjusted to the Arena Eternal like a hog to mud.

Biker always goes for a plasma gun, and he can almost always be found in its vicinity. It's his first choice to grab and his first choice to use. Biker is completely unrefined and without manners, and even his praise is a slap at best.

Patriot

When cybronic enhancements became the rage, the line of distinction between life and death became blurred. Patriot found this amusing, simply because he had walked that line for years. A vampire, Patriot is neither truly alive nor completely dead, but is an undead being preying on the living for food. Cybronic implants give him additional power and strength to complement his already incredible abilities, and give him new methods by which he can drain the life of his victims. Still a creature of his cravings, Patriot now hungers for victory instead of simple sustenance.

Patriot likes using the plasma gun and generally seeks it out in most situations. He also likes to take the Quad, especially when he can use it with his favorite weapon. He generally views anyone else he fights as less of an opponent and more of a snack for later, but it's hard not to like his approach regardless.

Anarki

Most of the combatants in the Arena Eternal are older than Anarki, but that doesn't bother him. He made his name as an enforcer for the Random Access gang. Once upon a time, Anarki had his own personality and his own memories. Now, thanks to the constant downloads of cybronic software, the real Anarki has been blended with the stolen ideas from thousands of people and memories of battles both real and virtual. There's no distinction in Anarki's mind between the virtual world and the real world. In fact, his cybronic implants make the world through Anarki's eyes appear like the virtual world he's most comfortable in.

Anarki goes through just about anything to get his hands on a shotgun, including you. It is far and away his favorite weapon. He also always attempts to get the two power-ups that appear in his arena. Anarki has little respect for anything but himself and doesn't take losing well.

THE FIFTH TIER ENEMIES

RAZOR

After the invasion of Stroggos, things on Earth were out of control. The troops of the Terran Coalition couldn't cover all of the hotspots at once. Local militia groups, and even biker gangs, took over and kept at least a semblance of order in many trouble spots. It was in spots like this that Razor made a name for himself. Never officially commended, or even commissioned, many towns in the Pacific Northwest owe their continued existence to Razor and his gang of Roto-Ryders.

Razor is very aggressive but will break off a failed attack to keep himself alive if necessary. He also loves to snipe. The BFG10K is far and away his weapon of choice if he can locate one. Razor is much smarter than his background might imply, and he rarely takes himself seriously in victory or defeat.

VISOR

Warrior clones populate the Arena Eternal. Many come from the line of Visor, a Terran cyborg created and bred for fighting and killing. Where some believe Visor was synthesized from the DNA of countless Terran warriors throughout history, others believe he is simply one of the great Terran heroes himself. Visor knows the truth, and he's not telling anyone. His entire reason for being is combat, and he is very good at his job.

Visor is very aggressive and quite likely to hold a grudge against a particular opponent. He tends to be pretty honorable, though, and rarely kills an enemy who is chatting. The rocket launcher, followed by the railgun, is his favorite weapon. Visor is a no-nonsense competitor, and his comments reflect his concentration on battle.

Stripe

When you come from the streets, staying away from the gangbangers and the drug pushers isn't easy. Stripe did some hard time anyway, but he did it to protect his brother, who wasn't smart enough or tough enough to survive in the joint. It didn't help, however, and Stripe's brother ended up six feet under. They discovered that Stripe was covering for his brother and offered him a deal—stay in prison or go fight. Stripe chose to fight and wound up in the Arena Eternal.

While Stripe is an excellent warrior, he is more concerned with his own preservation than scoring frags. This may be a large part of the reason he favors the BFG, the Quad, and the battle suit, since these items allow him to either clear the area quickly (which prevents retaliation) or keep him safe. Stripe is confident but not too cocky when he speaks.

Keel

Lance Corporal Ben Keel of the Terran Commonwealth Special Forces was killed on Subic 3 during the Spiker Insurrection as he attempted to rout a nest of rebel artillery. Six months later, Keel was born. A cybronically-enhanced warrior, Keel is a product of alien bioengineering and Terran refinements. While Keel appears to be a human head mounted on a suit of powered armor, he is much more than simply a battle bot. He's also substantially less than human. His programming instructs him to fight and kill without mercy or regard for his own safety. This is not to say that he doesn't defend himself, but Keel's instincts and his hardwired code suggest that the best way to prevent dying is to eliminate all opposition.

In many ways, Keel is the opposite of Stripe. He is almost totally geared for the attack and rarely breaks off combat once it starts. The railgun is his preferred method of destruction, and he is more than competent with it. Keel doles out his respect grudgingly.

Uriel

Before humans came to the Arena Eternal, Uriel reigned here. Alleged to be descended from the Arena Masters themselves, Uriel and his race have inspired lesser creatures to run in terror from their vicious claws. For eons, nothing less than the Masters themselves dared to challenge Uriel. Now, this powerful gargoyle grows tired of combat and constant conflict. While he yearns for the release that death will bring, he still must defend himself to the death. Only one truly worthy of assuming his mantle can progress past him, and this is not a mantle he will give up easily.

Uriel protects himself when necessary but is prone to fits of rage against a particular opponent. The lightning gun and the plasma gun are his tools of choice, but he won't hesitate to find and use a BFG if one is available. Uriel's speeches indicate both his desire to die and his equal desire to conquer.

The Sixth Tier and the Final Level Enemies

Bones

Bones is a testament to the awesome power of the Arena Masters. Reputed to have been created from the bones of a long-dead warrior, Bones is an animated skeleton, even more a member of the undead than Patriot or Cadavre. The burning question in the minds of anyone facing Bones is, "Where do the gibs come from?"

Bones, as an artificial undead construction, has never been truly alive and has no idea of what life is like. Even more than Orbb, Bones is unaffected by the pain and suffering of others. He is an excellent warrior with any weapon.

CADAVRE

Certainly the most evil creature to populate the Arena Eternal is Cadavre, an animated corpse bent on continuing the destruction he wrought in life. A convicted murderer many times over, no one is sure the exact number of victims Cadavre claimed in his lifetime. It is known that during a prison break, he wiped out a baker's dozen of victims, including eight other inmates and three anti-death penalty protesters camped outside the prison. Cadavre is a bloated and evil creature, still dressed in his prison orange, whose sagging innards hang from his distended belly. There is nothing good left in Cadavre, if there ever was anything good to begin with.

Despite his obviously evil bent, Cadavre isn't particularly vengeful or aggressive. He's also not concerned with self-preservation. He generally prefers to work with a rocket launcher, turning his opponents into the gibs that resemble his body. His speech is gross and disgusting, almost as much as his physical appearance.

DOOM

The last transmission from Doom to Earth from Mars was, "They're all dead, every last fraggin' one of 'em." Everything after that was just unintelligible screaming. When the team from Earth finally did set down on Mars, all they found were the remains of the marine strike team and researchers. There were no demons remaining. There was also no trace of Doom. The Arena Masters had claimed him as one of their own.

Doom likes to camp out and snipe, which is the main reason that the railgun is his preferred weapon. He loves the Quad as well, and happily uses a BFG if there is one available on the map. His speech is somewhat disordered, and it seems at times that he might be fighting a different battle than his opponents, although this doesn't prevent him from being deadly.

MAJOR

Major Artemis Wayland is haunted by the fallen comrades from the Stroggos campaign. She lost everything and everyone to the onrushing hordes of cyborgs, and because of this, she has refused any cybronic implants herself. She bears the scars of thousands of conflicts and wears them proudly, refusing even to cover up the socket where her eye was lost to a combat long past. While still fully human, Major Wayland is a killing machine bent on recovering the honor she lost to the Stroggs.

Major is most at home with a rocket launcher, which she uses with deadly effect. While she is competent with other weapons, this one is her favorite. Major's comments are generally short and to the point.

SORLAG

The reptilian Sorlag of the Sorg Clan is the ultimate in unprincipled mercenaries. She'd not only sell her own mother for a buck, she'd sell her in pieces if it were more profitable that way. Any way she can get an unfair advantage, she'll take. Sorlag wasn't against making a few credits selling off bits and pieces of human savages to Cyborgers, a fact that has earned her a number of powerful enemies. Of course, that also gave her nearly limitless battlefield experience, as well as a love for dis-memberment and death.

Sorlag's main weapons of choice are the shotgun and the railgun. She happily uses either, but she prefers to kill with the shotgun up close and personal. Sorlag can often be seen fighting with Doom over any Quad that appears on a given level. Sorlag's sibilant-filled speech is loaded with anger and hatred of anything but herself.

XAERO

No one is more deadly than the mutant Xaero. His entire being is centered on death and destruction. Countless victories in the Arena Eternal have made him the ultimate master of the carnage he surveys. Xaero claims to be able to see into the minds of his opponents, allowing him to guess their next move and kill them before they can kill him. He is unbeaten in the arenas, and this has made him brash. Xaero is definitely not overconfident though—he can do what he says. Xaero is the true master of the *Quake III Arena* universe, firing with deadly accuracy and attacking with lightning speed. Only the best ever see him, and only the true masters survive his onslaught.

Xaero is aggressive and vengeful and takes any insult very personally. However, he's not so battle-mad that he won't break off combat to heal if need be. He likes the railgun and the BFG, and if available, he'll hunt down the invisibility icon. Xaero respects very little, so any praise he gives you is earned indeed.

5 QUAKE

The Introduction level and the first tier arenas

ARENA

> **Note**
>
> *Since you start with the gauntlet and machinegun every time you start a level or respawn after being killed, these two weapons appear in every arena.*

THE INTRODUCTION LEVEL

**SINGLE-PLAYER ENEMY:
CRASH WEAPONS: SHOTGUN,
PLASMA GUN POWER-UPS: NONE
FRAG LIMIT: 5**

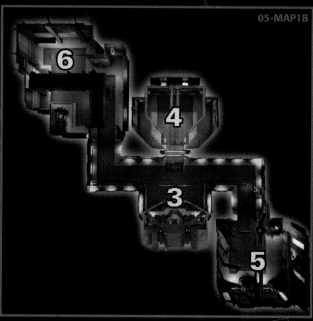

05-MAP1B

05-MAP1A

1. You enter the level here. Here you'll find a yellow armor, green health, and a shotgun.
2. The teleporter is located here.
3. Going through the teleporter takes you to this spot.
4. You'll find a second shotgun in this room.
5. An additional set of yellow armor is located here.
6. The plamsa gun, armor shards, and more can be found in this area.

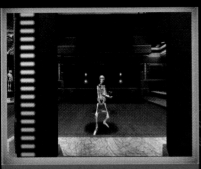

Check yourself in the mirror to see what your opponents will be looking at as you gun them down.

If you wish, you can get a little practice in before tackling the main arenas in *Quake III Arena*. This simple arena teaches you some of the basics of playing *Quake III Arena* and introduces you to several important items. You arrive in a small room facing a mirror. Take a look at yourself before exploring the surrounding area.

In the room with you is a suit of yellow armor and some green health. Also nab the shotgun before running through the teleporter across the room from where you started.

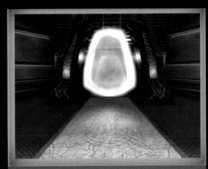

This teleporter takes you to the main area of this arena.

You appear directly in front of a door, next to a gold health. Go through the door and pick up another shotgun, as well as two more green health crosses. When you are ready, turn and leave through the door back to where you teleported in.

The small room in the middle of the level holds another shotgun.

Go left from the inside of the shotgun room. The hall opens up at the end, revealing a yellow health and a second suit of yellow armor. Get the armor, and if you've been wounded, be sure to pick up the yellow health.

The yellow health restores 25 points if you've been wounded, while the yellow armor prevents some damage.

Run back through the middle hallway to the other side of the map. This is the most useful area on this training level, thanks to the box of shotgun shells, two more yellow healths, the plasma gun, and three armor shards. You should be able to hold this area for a little while, using the health when you get damaged, and picking up the plasma gun to replace the cells you use.

This area contains a number of items, all worth grabbing and trying out. The shotgun ammunition is particularly useful on this tiny map.

Arena Gate

SINGLE-PLAYER ENEMY: RANGER
WEAPONS: SHOTGUN, ROCKET LAUNCHER, PLASMA GUN
POWER-UPS: NONE
FRAG LIMIT: 10

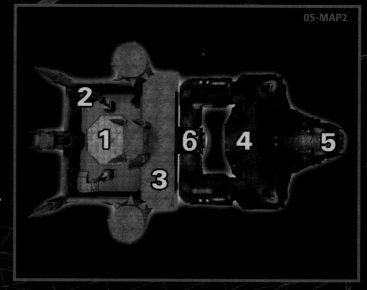

05-MAP2

1. The rocket launcher is located in the middle of this courtyard.
2. Two yellow health sits on this small set of stairs.
3. The shotgun is located at this bend in the hallway, beneath this roof.
4. The plasma gun and two yellow health appear here.
5. The red armor appears in the back of the demonic mouth.
6. A gold health sits at hallway T.

This level contains two major sections, the rocket launcher courtyard and the plasma gun room. The rocket launcher courtyard contains two yellow health crosses and six armor shards, making it a very powerful area. The armor shards are located behind the statues on either side of the courtyard, which offers some protection from the center of the courtyard when snagging them. Both of the yellow healths appear on one of the small staircases in the corner of the room.

Through the corridors connecting the two main areas, you can find a gold health and the shotgun. The main corridor leading from the rocket launcher courtyard is dangerous simply because it is long and straight, making it easy for an enemy to kill you by pursuing you or waiting in the courtyard.

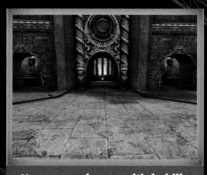

You can rack up multiple kills waiting for your enemies to come down the main hallway to the rocket launcher courtyard.

In the plasma gun room, there's ammunition, which is useful, but not critical on this level. More importantly, the plasma gun itself rests in the center of the room. It's a simple task to run from one side to the other and snag the plasma gun as you go across and back to the connecting corridors.

Armor shards appear between the statues and the walls while yellow health appears on the staircase in the back. The focus of this area is the rocket launcher in the middle.

Tip

There are also two yellow health in this room, straight through the left entrance.

Run a straight line through this room to get the plasma gun and head back to the corridors leading to the rocket launcher courtyard.

The back half of the plasma gun room is dominated by the gigantic mouth. The stairs up to it appear to lead into the mouth itself, but the gigantic fangs block the entrance from the sides fairly effectively. It's very easy to get caught on them. Instead, run straight up the tongue to get the red armor at the back.

The red body armor is the prize of running into the demonic mouth.

Once you have the red armor, you've got to get out of the mouth quickly, or you're dead. The back of the mouth offers limited protection, but since the two main weapons on this level—the rocket launcher and the plasma gun—can create tremendous splash damage, the protection here is really only against direct hits. You're still very vulnerable to being killed with indirect fire.

Even though you have some protection here, don't linger in the back of the mouth for too long.

While the plasma gun room is important, most of the action takes place in the rocket launcher courtyard. In fact, the area where the rocket launcher appears is an excellent camping spot. Because your enemies are moving to this room constantly, they must head up the long corridor toward you, offering you several shots at them as they approach. Listen for the sound of someone grabbing a weapon (the shotgun) nearby. When you hear it, that enemy almost always enters the courtyard through the portal on the right. Also keep your ears open for the sounds of an enemy respawning close by. The most common respawning locations in this area are on the small staircase in the back right and just behind the entrance to the left.

The gold health located in the middle of the arena is extremely important. It's easier to protect from the rocket launcher courtyard because you can keep your eye on it. If an enemy is camping out in the rocket launcher courtyard, grab this health and run in. Use the statues on the sides as cover as you fire, preferably with the plasma gun.

When you hear the shotgun picked up, look right and fire.

The statues make excellent cover when this room is being guarded.

It's also quite possible to camp by the red armor, although you are advised not to do so in the mouth itself. This is an important area to protect because of the armor, the 50 points of health, and the plasma gun. Keep your ears open for the sounds of approaching enemies. The best way to tell which direction your enemy is coming from is to listen for the sound of ammunition being picked up. When you hear it, your enemy almost always enters this room from the right side.

Keep your eye trained on the left entrance, but switch to the right when you hear the ammunition picked up.

House of Pain

SINGLE-PLAYER ENEMY: PHOBOS
WEAPONS: SHOTGUN, ROCKET LAUNCHER, PLASMA GUN
POWER-UP: HASTE
FRAG LIMIT: 10

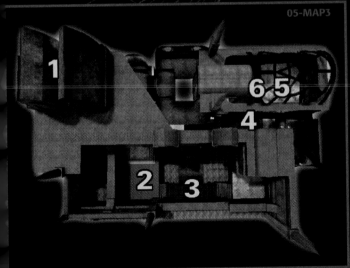

05-MAP3

1. The rocket launcher room is beneath this large roof.
2. Yellow armor appears here.
3. The plasma gun is located in the center of this group of staircases.
4. The red armor appears in the water area here.
5. The haste icon appears here.
6. You can find the shotgun overlooking the red armor in this spot.

This level consists of several significant areas. The most notable are the watery basement, the rocket launcher room, the plasma gun courtyard, and the haste room. The water area lies below the haste icon and can be accessed from either side or the bridge. This same corridor opens into the plasma courtyard and leads directly to the plasma gun. The rocket launcher room lies off to the side of the upper corridors connecting the haste room to the plasma gun courtyard.

The rocket launcher room is interesting because it offers an extremely powerful weapon but is itself something of a trap. The only way into and out of this room is through the large door. The room itself contains only the rocket launcher and machine gun ammunition, so it's difficult to stay in here for too long. The two side alcoves make excellent sniping positions in this room, and the ledges along the walls can be reached by rocket jumping, making for a unique vantage point.

Tip

Listen for the sound of the door opening. When you hear it, you know that someone is going after the rocket launcher and must come back through the door eventually.

The rocket launcher has no health around it and is a dead-end room. There's only one way out.

The rocket launcher has some interesting sniping positions if you use a rocket jump.

The watery basement area is another dead end. You can enter it from the plasma gun courtyard or from the upper level by the haste icon, but there is only one fast way out. It is possible to jump on the small wall ledges next to the red body armor and climb out of this area, but this is time consuming and leaves you very vulnerable to attack. The best and fastest way out is to run through to the plamsa gun courtyard.

Tip

Listen for the sound of an enemy grabbing the red armor. Chances are this enemy will emerge in the plasma gun courtyard and be a sitting duck for an ambush.

The plasma gun courtyard is a wide-open area with three main exits. The first is the central path, which leads directly to the watery corridor. When facing this passage, the left path out of the courtyard leads to the rocket launcher room. The right path heads over to the haste area and the bridge. This is an extremely beneficial area because it contains a great weapon, a gold health, yellow armor, and several boxes of ammunition. However, since it is easily accessible from any other point on the map, it is difficult to defend.

The red armor is tempting, but getting it forces you to move in one of two directions. Either way leaves you open to attack.

Climbing the wall near the red armor is faster than running through the corridor, but it leaves you much more open to being fragged.

The final major area is the haste platform. This lies just above the red body armor and is connected by corridors to the rocket launcher room and the plasma gun courtyard. The central bridge leads to the shotgun. It's tempting to guard this area by standing in the back corner just behind where the haste icon appears. However, since the two entrances to this area are far apart, it's difficult to watch them both at the same time.

The plasma gun courtyard contains many useful items, but it does not have many good sniping locations.

The haste icon is deadly on this small level since your enemy is never far away.

Tip

The plasma gun and the haste power-up form the most powerful weapon combination in this arena. Note that additional plasma ammunition appears near the haste icon. With both of these items working, you are nearly unstoppable.

Be aware of the sound of someone grabbing the armor shards. There are two located just off the haste area, and there's a set of five located between the rocket launcher room and the haste area. When you hear them picked up, you'll know exactly where your enemy is located.

Tip

To confuse your enemies, grab only two of the five armor shards by the rocket launcher room. This causes them to think you are in the other armor shard location, allowing you to sneak in for a kill.

The shotgun appears on the platform across the bridge from the haste icon. From this location, you can see the red body armor in the water below.

The armor shards are important auditory clues in this arena.

Finally, when you hear someone in the water, run to the plasma gun courtyard as fast as you can. Almost every time, your enemy emerges here and is lined up perfectly for you. Arm yourself either with the plasma gun or the rocket launcher, and be ready to fire as soon as the enemy appears. While your opponent probably has the additional protection of the red armor, you have the element of surprise.

You can run from either of the other major areas to here in about the same amount of time as it takes to run through the watery basement. Set yourself up for a perfect ambush.

ARENA OF DEATH

SINGLE-PLAYER ENEMIES: MYNX, ORBB
WEAPONS: SHOTGUN, GRENADE LAUNCHER, ROCKET LAUNCHER, PLASMA GUN
POWER-UPS: NONE
FRAG LIMIT: 15

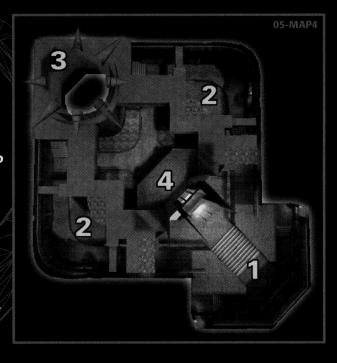

05-MAP4

1. The rocket launcher and plasma gun both arrive at this spot above the stairs.
2. Shotguns are located in these two corners of the map.
3. The grenade launcher shows up in this back corner.
4. The red armor appears in the alcove under the tower on top of the bridge.

This is an extremely tight level containing only a few major areas. The map is set up like a pair of interconnecting circles, one slightly smaller and higher up than the first. The larger, lower part of the arena is dominated by the huge staircase on one side of the map. The smaller circle overlooks the central area and contains red body armor.

The large staircase is the site of most of the fighting on this map. This is the most frequently defended place simply because of the power it offers. There are two gold healths in the immediate vicinity and a quartet of armor shards at the bottom of the stairs. More importantly, both the plasma gun and the rocket launcher appear at the center of the area on the top of the stairs. Each time the weapon here is grabbed, there is a 50-50 chance of either one spawning in next. Because of these weapons and the powerful health icons in the area, this part of the level, if guarded, is incredibly strong.

The top of the stairs contains powerful weapons and health and has armor shards nearby.

There is also a small outer ledge that runs around the level and leads to the upper portion. If you are on the lower ground, you must jump to reach this ledge. Run up the darkened staircase to find the grenade launcher, an excellent weapon to use from the bridge that spans the center of the map.

Shotguns are located in opposite corners of the map. Notice the higher ledge behind the shotgun. This leads to the grenade launcher and the red armor.

The grenade launcher is located across the map from the large staircase.

In the middle of the bridge in a small alcove, you find the red body armor. This is an excellent sniping location, since it is protected from the large staircase on the one side and offers a tremendous view of the rest of the level.

The red armor lies in an open alcove at the center of the map.

With the red armor and a good weapon, you can protect almost half of this map.

There are also two gold healths located in the area below the red body armor. While you are vulnerable to anyone on the bridge as you approach these healths, you are very well protected once you reach them. This area cannot be seen by anyone on either the bridge above or the main staircase.

If you need them, the two gold healths located under the red armor alcove are a welcome sight.

Powerstation 0218

SINGLE-PLAYER ENEMY: SARGE
WEAPONS: SHOTGUN, ROCKET LAUNCHER
POWER-UPS: QUAD, REGENERATION
FRAG LIMIT: 10

1. The Quad and the regeneration icons both arrive on the symbol here.
2. The rocket launcher room is here.
3. The shotgun is here.
4. A suit of yellow armor rests here.

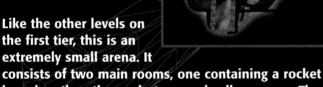

05-MAP5

Like the other levels on the first tier, this is an extremely small arena. It consists of two main rooms, one containing a rocket launcher, the other a shotgun and yellow armor. These rooms are connected by a set of corridors that also branches out to a power-up area.

The rocket launcher room is something of a dead end. There is only one corridor that leads in and out of it. However, since there is a central pillar in the middle of the room, you have a slightly better chance of escaping with little or no damage should someone approach and attack you. The pair of yellow healths on the other side of the column can help if you do take damage.

The rocket launcher room contains only one exit. You often have to fight your way out of here.

The shotgun room is a little more accessible since it has two corridors that lead out of it. The main corridor connects it to the rocket launcher room and has a suit of yellow combat armor near it. The corridor off to the side leads to the power-up room and connects back into the main corridor about halfway through. There is some additional ammunition in the hall leading between this room and the power-up room. The shotgun room also contains both a yellow health and a gold health, making it an excellent destination when you are wounded.

The power-up room holds only power-ups on this level. There is a 50 percent chance of either a Quad or a regeneration icon appearing here. Naturally, on a level of this size, the Quad is incredibly powerful, especially with the rocket launcher in the narrow corridors. As you head back into the main corridor, you find some additional health.

The shotgun room contains a lot of health, but the two entrances make it difficult to defend.

The presence of the yellow armor in this room makes it a popular destination.

Both the Quad and the regeneration icon appear on this level, both in the same spot. There's an equal chance for either one at any time.

There is additional health in the corridor leading from the power-up room to the main hallway between the weapon rooms.

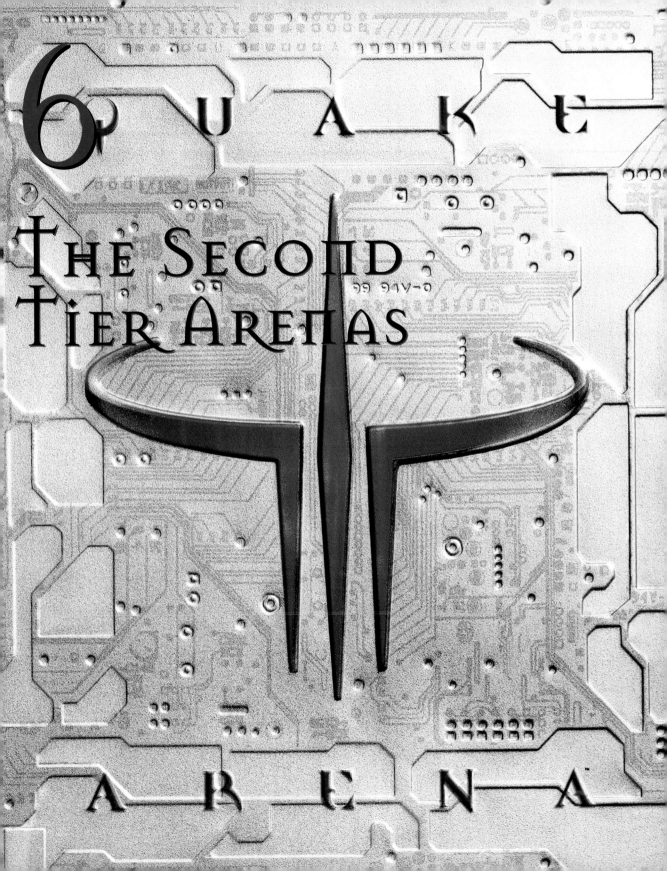

6 Quake

The Second Tier Arenas

ARENA

The Place of Many Deaths

SINGLE-PLAYER ENEMIES: ORBB, BITTERMAN, GRUNT
WEAPONS: SHOTGUN, ROCKET LAUNCHER, PLASMA GUN
POWER-UPS: QUAD
FRAG LIMIT: 20

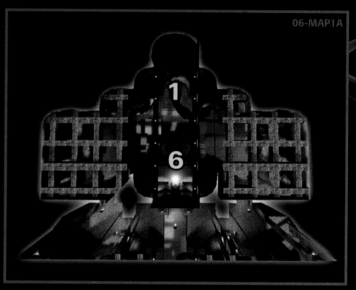

06-MAP1A

1. The red armor is located in the fog here.
2. The rocket launcher is on the back of the platform here.
3. The teleporter is here.
4. The plasma gun is sitting across from the teleporter here.
5. The Quad appears on the lowest floor here, under the bridge to the rocket launcher.
6. The teleporter from number 3 takes you here, facing the Quad area.

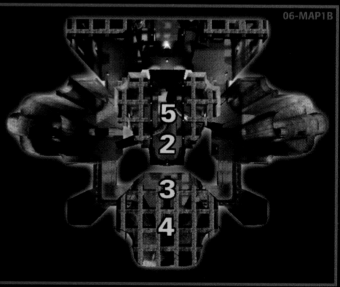

06-MAP1B

This is the first level that has significant upper and lower parts. The key areas here are the massive staircase that leads up to the rocket launcher, the back hallway containing the plasma gun and a teleporter, the front corridor that holds health and the Quad power-up, and the low fog bank that contains the red body armor.

Tip

A lot of the combat takes place in the fog bank, fighting over the red armor. You can stay out of this conflict and still get a few kills by sniping from the large staircase above this area.

There are a few ways in to the red armor. You can go down the staircase, which leads right to both the armor and a yellow health. You can also drop in from the staircase on either side of this low alcove. However, short of rocket jumping, the stairs are the only way out of the fog bank, which leaves you vulnerable to enemy attacks.

The red armor is easy to get, but it's not always simple to escape the fog bank.

Straight ahead up the stairs from the fog bank is the main corridor, which contains the Quad. The Quad appears at the junction of the three corridors here, making it easy to reach from virtually anywhere. Naturally, combat often centers on this area, especially when the Quad is present. Head up from the fog bank and turn right where the Quad appears, then run to the end of the hallway. You can protect the Quad from this small, dark alcove.

The Quad appears at the junction of three hallways, making it easily accessible and constantly fought over.

You can protect the Quad from this small alcove. The plasma gun is perfectly suited for this task.

You can also run down either of the side hallways to the back corridor. This corridor contains the plasma gun. The teleporter here leads to the area just above the fog bank, and regardless of which side of the teleporter you run through, you end up facing the Quad. There is also a gold health behind the teleporter.

The final area, which contains a lot of the carnage for this level, is the huge staircase that dominates the area near the fog bank. Both sides of the staircase lead to the same platform that overlooks the fog. Head down the catwalk to find the rocket launcher on the far side. This rocket launcher platform is located above the Quad, which makes it another good area to camp.

The location of the gold health behind the teleporter is important. Since you can run through this teleporter in either direction, it allows for a quick escape from this area.

You can guard this area for short periods of time, but the lack of health makes it difficult to stay here for too long.

Running through the teleporter puts you back in the main hallways facing the Quad. The red armor is directly behind you.

Tip

If you want an even better camping location, you can rocket jump to the veins dangling from the ceiling over this area. You don't have a tremendous field of view of the lower level below, but you can protect the rocket launcher easily from here, and the element of surprise is often good for a couple of frags.

THE FORGOTTEN PLACE

SINGLE-PLAYER ENEMIES: HOSSMAN, DAEMIA
WEAPONS: SHOTGUN, GRENADE LAUNCHER, ROCKET LAUNCHER, PLASMA GUN
POWER-UPS: NONE
FRAG LIMIT: 15

06-MAP2

1. The rocket launcher is located in a narrow alcove here.
2. Red armor can be found at the end of the catwalk.
3. The shotgun is here, overlooking the fog bank.
4. This area is covered in yellowish fog.
5. The grenade launcher is located on the bridge in this corner.
6. The plasma gun is here.
7. A suit of yellow armor is here.

This is by far the most complicated level you have encountered so far. While it isn't extremely large, it is quite convoluted, with staircases leading in many different directions. There are several wide-open areas with ammunition and weapons along the side walls, as well as a catwalk that runs over much of the map area. Additionally, there is a lower, fog-encased section that holds little of value but connects to most of the rest of the level.

This map is marked by large, open areas with little in the way of cover.

Tip

This level is extremely open, making it difficult to snipe. Keep moving and try not to get pinned down. While this level is a little larger than you are used to, all of the areas are easily accessible, making the battle extremely fluid.

The rocket launcher is hard to get because of its location on this level.

Tip

The ceiling of the rocket launcher alcove is actually the catwalk that leads across the center of the level. Therefore, you can drop off the bridge into this alcove, and you can rocket jump up to the bridge after getting the rocket launcher. Both tactics reduce the amount of time you need to spend in this area. Should you rocket jump, there is health nearby on the bridge.

Naturally, the rocket launcher is highly sought after on this level, but getting it is extremely difficult and dangerous. It's located in a small and narrow alcove, making it difficult to get in and out without being hammered by an enemy.

Tip

Up on the bridge, you can find the grenade launcher, which is an excellent weapon from this height. Use it to drop grenades to the lower level, through doorways, and especially into the rocket launcher alcove. This keeps anyone else from grabbing it. If you follow the bridge to the end, you can find a suit of red armor.

Important sound cues on this level include the four armor shards near the plasma gun and the two near the shotgun by the main courtyard. The plasma gun is located in a small side courtyard below the catwalk. Another important sound cue is the bounce pad at one end of the fog. If you hear the bounce pad close by, head to it. The physics of the bounce pad make whoever launches from it relatively vulnerable at the top of its arc.

The plasma gun is located in a small but easily accessible courtyard.

Health and ammunition are located throughout this level. There are several gold healths; the most notable one is just up the stairs in the middle of the low fog bank. Other than that, there is little of value in the fog.

The catwalk that spans the level contains many useful items, like the grenade launcher and a suit of red body armor.

This gold health just out of the fog is the most useful item in this area.

You can also find a suit of yellow armor in the twisting, open corridors of this arena

Tip

The upper and lower areas of this map are of almost identical size. If you see someone heading in a particular direction on a different level, head the same way and you can almost always reach the next courtyard at the same time.

THE CAMPING GROUNDS

SINGLE-PLAYER ENEMIES: ORBB, HOSSMAN, DAEMIA, BITTERMAN, GRUNT
WEAPONS: SHOTGUN, ROCKET LAUNCHER, RAILGUN, PLASMA GUN
POWER-UPS: QUAD, PERSONAL TELEPORTER, MEGA-HEALTH
FRAG LIMIT: 20

1. The Quad appears here.
2. Jump on the bounce pad to find the rocket launcher on this high ledge.
3. There is a suit of yellow armor here.
4. There is a large cache of ammunition at the bottom of the stairs.
5. The railgun platform is here.
6. The plasma gun appears here.
7. Red armor is located here.
8. The Mega-Health appears on this shelf.
9. The personal teleporter is here.
10. This shelf holds a large cache of ammunition.
11. The shotgun is here.

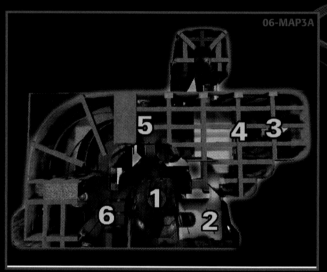

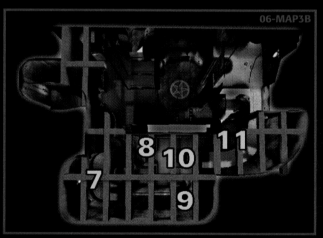

If you are the type of *Quake*™ player who likes to sit in one spot and wait for your enemies to run past, this is the map that you have been waiting for. This level is loaded with spots that are perfect for sitting tight and sniping at anyone who passes by.

This level is dominated by several staircases. One of these holds a set of yellow armor at the top. Above it, a bridge crosses the area below. This bridge makes a good vantage point for the staircase and the yellow armor, as well as the floor on the approach to the stairs. The bottom of the stairs contains a wealth of ammunition, making it one of the more useful areas, as long as no one is sniping from above.

Unfortunately, the bridge isn't that safe. Overlooking it is a small platform containing both the railgun and railgun slugs. This area overlooks a small section of the stairs leading to the yellow armor and the large bridge. This is a very powerful camping location, and you can score a number of kills from here.

This level contains a wealth of camping locations, like this spot overlooking the yellow armor.

The bottom of the stairs with the yellow armor holds a yellow health and four types of ammunition.

At the very center of the map, you can find the Quad. This is an extremely accessible location, reachable from virtually anywhere on the level in just a few seconds. It is also extremely close to the plasma gun, which can be found just outside of the Quad area through the central doorway.

This bounce pad leads up to the railgun, which is situated in the prime sniping location on this level. You can score a number of kills from here.

Tip

This area is accessible only by the bounce pad. If you are sniping here, keep your ears open. When you hear the bounce pad, either turn and fire or drop off the platform to the floor below.

Tip

For another powerful combination, grab the Quad, then use the bounce pad behind it to reach the high platform with the rocket launcher.

Grab the rocket launcher and turn to face the wall. Notice the demonic face here. Turn right and follow the bridge to the end. There is a short series of jumps to pillars here loaded with ammunition, the personal teleporter, a Mega-Health, and the suit of red body armor. You can also reach this area from the bounce pad located below the red armor. If you jump off to the right of the red armor, you come down next to the bounce pad that leads up to the railgun.

The rocket launcher looks down over the Quad. You can also score the plasma gun by running through the doorway next to the Quad and moving slightly left.

Run straight from here to reach the collection of valuable items. This is an excellent place to guard, thanks to the immediate proximity of armor, health, and ammunition.

Tip

If you control your jump to the railgun, you can land on the small ledge—another perfect sniper's post.

The central level of this map consists mainly of corridors that connect the top and bottom areas. There isn't
much in terms of weaponry or ammunition, but you can
find a lot of health here. Small alcoves and ledges
make interesting sniping positions in this area.

Aside from the railgun, your best camping position is by
the rocket launcher. This gives you an excellent vantage
point to protect the Quad; sits you within easy reach of
ammunition, the Mega-Health, and the red armor; and
overlooks a frequently traveled area. Another area that
experiences heavy traffic is the spot just outside the
Quad location, which contains the plasma gun.

Keep your eyes open for these
useful green healths.

THE PROVING
GROUNDS

**SINGLE-PLAYER ENEMY:
HUNTER
WEAPONS: SHOTGUN, ROCKET
LAUNCHER, LIGHTNING GUN
POWER-UPS: NONE
FRAG LIMIT: 10**

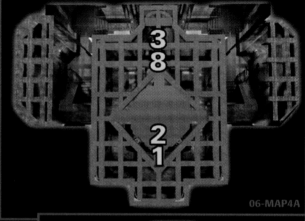

06-MAP4A

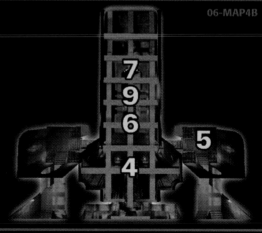

06-MAP4B

1. There is a suit of yellow armor on
   the highest floor here.
2. The rocket launcher is located directly
   beneath the yellow armor at number 1.
3. There is a teleporter here.
4. The lightning gun is here.
5. Shotguns can be found in these
   locations.
6. There is a second suit of yellow
   armor here.
7. The second teleporter is here.
8. You arrive here from the teleporter at
   number 3.
9. You arrive here from the teleporter at
   number 7.

This is a tight level with only a couple of significant areas. The central area contains two main levels, one with armor, the other with ammunition and the rocket launcher. The other significant area is the lightning gun corridor.

This small level is effectively one large, vertical room with two sets of corridors branching off from it. The bottom of the central area is significant because of the rocket launcher. All three of the bounce pads here lead back to the top level. The two corner ones take you directly to the corners of the top room, while the third pad takes you through the teleporter.

The rocket launcher is crucial to success on this level. The side areas are narrow, allowing for significant splash damage.

Use the bounce pad on the other side of the pillar from the rocket launcher to reach the teleporter.

On the top level, the most significant feature is the teleporter. On the other side of the central pillar is a suit of yellow armor, while there is one gold health just below the teleporter. To either side, you can find five armor shards.

Jump through the teleporter to appear in the lightning gun corridor. You find a gold health and a suit of yellow armor here. At the end of the corridor, where it branches both to the left and right, a small alcove contains the lightning gun. This is an excellent weapon for this level because of the generally close quarters with your enemies.

This suit of yellow armor keeps you protected from enemy attacks.

It's easy to overlook this gold health because you need to go out of your way to get it.

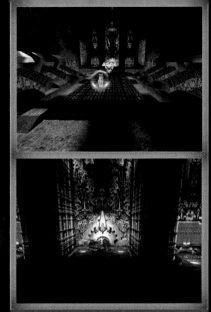

The lightning gun corridor contains 50 points each of health and armor, as well as the lightning gun itself.

Watch out for the fog of death! Falling in will kill you and strip you of a frag.

Both of the side corridors from the top and bottom of the central room lead to the same places, and both the top and bottom branches on each side connect to each other. Heading through the corridor where the upper and lower sides meet takes you through the lightning gun corridor. You can access the teleporter from this side. Doing so auto-matically dumps you back to the bottom of the central pillar on the opposite side from the rocket launcher.

Tip

The fall from the teleporter always strips a point or two of health from you. Don't do this if you are nearly dead.

In the side passages, the landing on one side holds a shotgun while the other holds four armor shards. Both of these landings also contain yellow health.

The two landings up from the lightning gun corridor hold health and other useful items.

Tip

Since this is a small level rich in ammunition, health, and armor, deny these things to your opponent. Shooting a rocket into a wall near you strips off a point or two of health, allowing you to snag the yellow and gold crosses, keeping them from your opponent's grasp.

Quake

The Third Tier Arenas

Arena

Temple of Retribution

SINGLE-PLAYER ENEMIES: DAEMIA, WRACK, GRUNT, SLASH
WEAPONS: SHOTGUN, ROCKET LAUNCHER, RAILGUN, PLASMA GUN
POWER-UPS: QUAD, MEGA-HEALTH, PERSONAL TELEPORTER
FRAG LIMIT: 20

1. There is a rocket launcher on this bridge.
2. The personal teleporter is here.
3. Hit the wall button here to open the floor grate.
4. Drop through the grate to get the red armor.
5. The Quad appears here.
6. The railgun is located on this bridge.
7. You can find a suit of yellow armor near the lava here.
8. The teleporter and the Mega-Health are in a small room under the main level here.
9. The teleporter takes you here.
10. The plasma gun is here.
11. The shotgun and yellow armor are on the ledge here.
12. There is a second rocket launcher here.

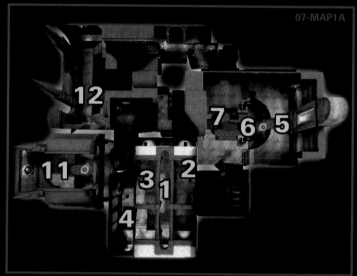

07-MAP1A

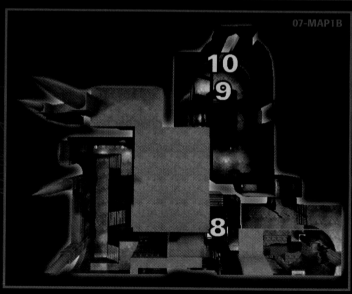

07-MAP1B

This level is larger than you are used to, with a number of important areas. There are two rocket launcher areas, one in the room, and one in the courtyard. Off to the side of the rocket launcher room is a shotgun area. There is a dungeon area and a huge open courtyard containing the Quad and a railgun, as well as a semi-secret area with a teleporter. Finally, there is a room with a decent amount of health and the plasma gun. This level flows well from one spot to the next, and it is easy to get from any one point to another. It feels much more compact than it really is.

The rocket launcher room is interesting because it contains multiple levels. There isn't much on the ground floor, but it's useful for moving from one side of the map to the other. Head up the stairs to find a gold health, then run across the catwalk for the rocket launcher, the personal teleporter, and a pair of yellow healths. Because it contains so much health and a powerful weapon, this is a common and excellent area to camp out in, particularly on the back side of the catwalk near where the personal teleporter appears.

If you press the button in the wall just past the two yellow healths, a grate in the floor opens up. Drop down and jump over the hole for the green health, then drop down. There's even more health down here, as well as ammunition and a suit of red armor. Run out through the automatic door.

Head up the stairs and get the rocket launcher. There's also a lot of health in the area, making this a great place to camp.

Note

This grate in the floor only opens from this side. You can't get to the red armor from the other side.

Tip

For a quick way out of this area, use the personal teleporter as soon as you grab the red armor.

Hit the wall button, then drop into this lower area. Grab the red armor and get out.

Run out of the area with the red armor, then turn left to find the second rocket launcher in the rocket launcher courtyard. There are armor shards up the stairs to the left and a suit of yellow armor up the stairs to the right. There's also a gold health on the ground below where the rocket launcher appears.

Either turn right from the door to the red armor or run straight through the lower area from the rocket launcher to get to the railgun courtyard. Run down the catwalk to grab the railgun, but be careful of falling off the sides since this drops you into the lava. The bounce pad at the bottom of the catwalk takes you directly up to the Quad.

You can also drop off the sides of the railgun catwalk near the top to a low platform with yellow health and yellow armor. Run through the short corridor here for some ammunition. Behind the teleporter, you find the Mega-Health.

Two views of the rocket launcher courtyard. Notice the placement of the gold health.

The railgun courtyard has a number of important items, including yellow armor, yellow health, and the Quad

Head through the teleporter to end up in the plasma gun room. With any luck, you'll land directly on the plasma gun itself. Grab the green health before leaving. The stairs down lead back to the rocket launcher courtyard. Heading out to the right leads to the same place, although from the top level instead of the ground. Going out the left door by the green health leads to the railgun courtyard.

After you get the yellow armor, run through the short corridor to the teleporter. Don't forget about the Mega-Health behind the teleporter before you leave.

Tip

You can see through the back of this teleporter. This is a very sneaky place to hide and gives you a perfect shot at anyone moving in to use the teleporter. If you've got the railgun, use it here.

The shotgun room connects the two rocket launcher areas on the top floor. Use the bounce pad to access the higher level, which contains health, armor, ammunition, and the shotgun. This is another excellent spot to snipe from because of its height, and because it is frequently traveled by enemies moving between the two rocket launchers.

The plasma gun and the green health make this a useful area. It's difficult to camp here because the teleporter brings enemies in quickly, but it's definitely worth running through.

The shotgun platform contains everything you need to score some frags and keep yourself safe.

You can make a lot of kills from the higher area as your enemies try to snag the items near the shotgun.

Tip

You can rocket jump from the shotgun platform to the next higher level, another good spot to snipe from because it is even higher up than the shotgun.

Brimstone Abbey

SINGLE-PLAYER ENEMIES: GORRE, BITTERMAN, SLASH, ANGEL
WEAPONS: SHOTGUN, GRENADE LAUNCHER, ROCKET LAUNCHER, RAILGUN, PLASMA GUN
POWER-UPS: QUAD, MEGA-HEALTH, INVISIBILITY
FRAG LIMIT: 20

07-MAP2A

1. The drowning pool containing red armor is here.
2. The railgun is here overlooking the drowning pool.
3. The Mega-Health is located in the fog bank here.
4. The shotgun is here.
5. Grenade launchers are on the balconies overlooking the cathedral area.
6. The Quad and invisibility power-ups appear here.
7. The plasma gun appears here.
8. The yellow armor is on a small ledge here.
9. There is more yellow armor here.
10. The rocket launcher is in the middle of this courtyard.
11. Health and armor shards appear in this small alcove.

This interesting level contains three major areas, the cathedral area, the rocket launcher courtyard, and the drowning pool. There is also a fog-shrouded area that contains some important artifacts. Because of the number of weapons and power-ups in this arena, battles have a tendency to get fast and furious.

Note

The water in the drowning pool was originally added to this level to demonstrate the water effects in **Quake III Arena.**

The drowning pool may be the most critical area on this map because so much of the action takes place here. It is heavily frequented because of the red armor, yellow health, and ammunition that lie in the bottom. The jump pad in the area leads up to a platform that overlooks the pool. The railgun here makes the perfect sniping weapon, and the amount of enemies that run through this area makes camping out here very tempting.

The railgun platform is excellent for sniping swimmers, but be careful of enemies sneaking in behind you.

The drowning pool is a powerful area and is heavily trafficked.

The cathedral area is also extremely important because it holds the two main power-ups on this level. Use the bounce pad here to reach the higher platform. Both the Quad and the invisibility icon appear here, with an equal chance for either one to appear at any given time.

The bounce pad takes you directly up to the power-up in the cathedral.

Tip

If you use air control on the bounce pad, you can reach the high ledges above the power-up area. There is machine gun ammo and gold health on either side. These platforms make excellent sniping posts.

There are other useful items near the cathedral as well. The plasma gun appears in the center of the room, and a stash of armor shards appears to one side. The ledges overlooking the sides of the cathedral area both contain grenade launchers—extremely useful for blasting anyone below.

There are three doors out of the main level of the cathedral area, one on a side wall and two across from the bounce pad. Both of these doors lead to the rocket launcher courtyard via another bounce pad at the end of the corridor. This is another useful area on this level. The rocket launcher appears in roughly the center of the room. There's also a small alcove containing two gold healths and four armor shards. The ledge at the back of the room contains green health and ammunition. The two paths off the ledge lead back to the balconies overlooking the cathedral.

The plasma gun is a good prize, especially if the Quad is available. Use the grenade launchers from the balconies next to the cathedral to kill anyone running inside.

Tip

Be careful going for the armor shards. The alcove makes you a sitting duck for an accurate shot with the rocket launcher.

This suit of armor requires a jump to get, but it's very useful when entering the heavily populated drowning pool.

The third door out of the cathedral leads to the foggy area that contains the shotgun. Down a side corridor with a dead end, you can also grab the Mega-Health. However, because the only way out of this area is the same way you came in, you are easily targeted by anyone pursuing you. The other end of the fog area connects to the drowning pool. Across the pool and up the stairs, there's a suit of yellow armor on a small ledge.

The bounce pad up from the cathedral takes you to the ledge holding the green health. The alcove is extremely valuable thanks to both the gold health and the armor shards.

The fog acts mainly as an artery for travelling between the more powerful areas. The presence of the Mega-Health more than makes up for the lack of other useful items.

QUAKE III ARENA
Prima's Official Strategy Guide

HERO'S KEEP

SINGLE-PLAYER ENEMIES: ANGEL, GORRE, WRACK, SLASH
WEAPONS: SHOTGUN, ROCKET LAUNCHER, RAILGUN, PLASMA GUN
POWER-UPS: MEGA-HEALTH
FRAG LIMIT: 20

1. Use the acceleration pad to grab the railgun on this ledge.
2. The secret bounce pad takes you through a line of health and armor shards.
3. The red armor is located on the beam over this room.
4. Shotguns are found in these locations.
5. The two plasma guns are located here.
6. Yellow armor is on the platform here.
7. The Mega-Health appears directly over this bounce pad.
8. The rocket launcher can be picked up after using the acceleration pad.

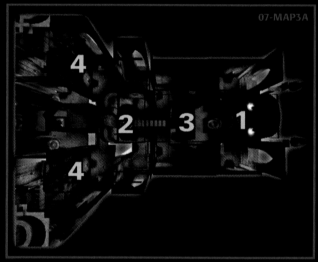

07-MAP3A

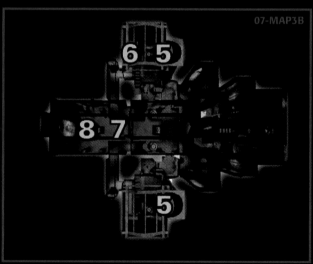

07-MAP3B

This interesting level is divided into two halves. On one side of the level, there's the rocket launcher, which is located on a vulnerable platform. On the other side, the railgun awaits, and a powerful line of armor and health can keep you viable. Connecting these two areas are corridors containing armor, health, shotguns, and plasma guns. This is a wild level due to the long, dangerous jumps and the tight conditions in the connecting corridors.

The rocket launcher is located at the far end of the first acceleration pad. Hop on to be thrown over to the small platform holding the rocket launcher. Between the two pads is the red fog that kills you if you fall into it. You're extremely vulnerable when you fly across, and a single hit with a good weapon can knock you into the fog. However, if you clear the central gap, you can air control yourself onto a secret bounce pad. To get back from the rocket launcher, use the second acceleration pad.

The acceleration pad propels you to the rocket launcher platform.

Tip

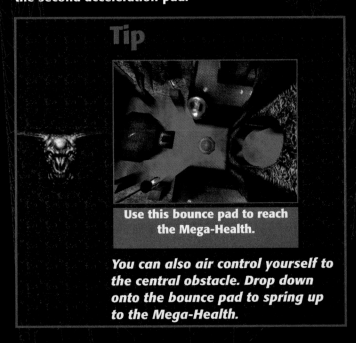

Use this bounce pad to reach the Mega-Health.

You can also air control yourself to the central obstacle. Drop down onto the bounce pad to spring up to the Mega-Health.

The two bounce pads in this area lead up to a catwalk that overlooks both this room and the connecting corridors. Explore these corridors thoroughly. There's a pair of shotguns in one set and two plasma guns in the next. Also check behind the statues for green health and armor shards. The statues also make excellent places to hide behind and use as cover from incoming fire.

The bounce pads lead you up to the higher ledges, which you can use to snipe at enemies running between the rocket launcher area and the railgun room.

QUAKE III ARENA
Prima's Official Strategy Guide

Tip

You can rocket jump up to the tops of the statues for an interesting sniping position.

On the other side of the map, the railgun platform awaits. Again, this powerful weapon is accessible only via the acceleration pad. Shoot over the fog and onto the high platform with the railgun. This weapon, the high vantage point, and the two yellow healths make this an excellent sniper's post. To get the red armor, drop straight down onto the bounce pad below the railgun and hop directly to it. This red armor platform is another excellent place to camp out, as are the two beams connecting it to the ceiling.

The connecting hallways also contain gold health and ammunition.

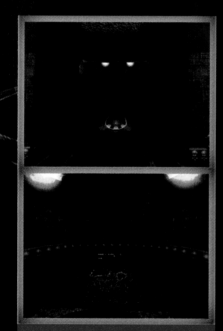

The acceleration pad here leads over the red armor to the railgun.

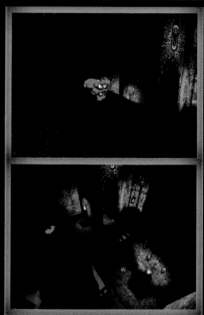

The red armor platform, and the beams on the sides of it, make excellent sniper's posts. This is especially effective if you have the railgun.

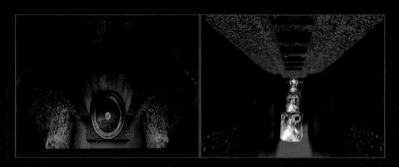

If you drop down the hole straight back from the accelerator pad, you find another bounce pad. This shoots you along a path containing rockets, armor shards, and a gold health. You bounce right onto the second bounce pad and up to the red armor.

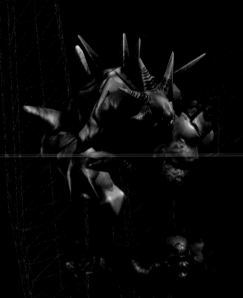

Interesting sniping positions abound on this level if you know where to look and have perfected your rocket jumping technique.

HELL'S GATE

SINGLE-PLAYER ENEMY: KLESK
WEAPONS: SHOTGUN, ROCKET LAUNCHER, RAILGUN, PLASMA GUN
POWER-UPS: BATTLE SUIT
FRAG LIMIT: 10

1. The rocket launcher is here.
2. Yellow armor and a plasma gun sit in this low room.
3. There is another plasma gun here.
4. The battle suit appears here.
5. The red armor appears at the bottom of the bridge under the higher level.
6. The railgun is here.

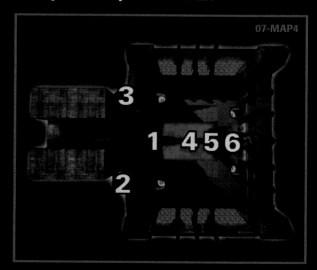

07-MAP4

The rocket launcher is a great weapon in this arena, partially because it can knock an enemy into the red fog.

This is a very simple map. It's perfect for two people since it consists of two very distinct halves and is extremely compact. Don't let the small size fool you, though. There's a lot packed into this little level.

The lower areas near the rocket launcher contain plasma guns, health, and armor.

On one side of the map, you have the name tower, which holds the rocket launcher at its center. On either side of this, on the lower level, there is a plasma gun. One of these small alcoves holds yellow armor while the other contains a gold health. The bounce pads in this area lead either back up to the rocket launcher or out to the two side ramps leading over to the other side.

These side ramps are important because they connect the two sides and contain ammunition. One of these ramps also holds a gold health while the other is home to a quartet of armor shards.

The side ramps hold some useful goodies, including armor shards and a gold health.

Tip

Don't be afraid of the red fog that lies between the ramps. You can safely jump from the top of the side ramps to the central ramp, or from the top of the central ramp to either side ramp.

The central ramp, which leads down from the rocket launcher to the area below the railgun, is where the battle suit appears. This is an extremely powerful power-up since it prevents the wearer from taking splash damage. When this suit is worn, your opponent must hit you with direct shots from both the rocket launcher and the plasma gun, which gives you a tremendous edge.

Get the battle suit to prevent your enemy from using several of his weapons effectively.

Tip

Because of the nature of the weapon, the grenade launcher can also be an effective sniping tool. While it is generally less accurate than other weapons, its ability to completely blanket an area with explosions should not be underrated.

Tip

If your enemy grabs the battle suit, use the railgun. It causes tremendous damage and doesn't deal splash damage anyway.

At the bottom of the central ramp, you find the suit of red armor and a pair of yellow healths. The bounce pads take you back up to the top level, where you can find the railgun overlooking the central ramp. Like the rocket launcher area, this side contains pillars that can be used as effective cover.

Don't pass up the red body armor.

This level is well-suited to duels with railguns. Use the nearby pillars to protect you.

Tip

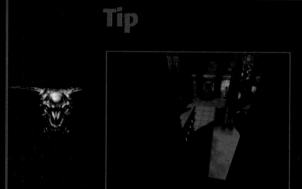

If you have the rocket launcher, you can rocket jump up to the high fortifications on the rocket launcher side of the map. If you are also equipped with the battle suit, it's even easier. This is an excellent sniping position since you can see most of the level and the pillars act as excellent cover.

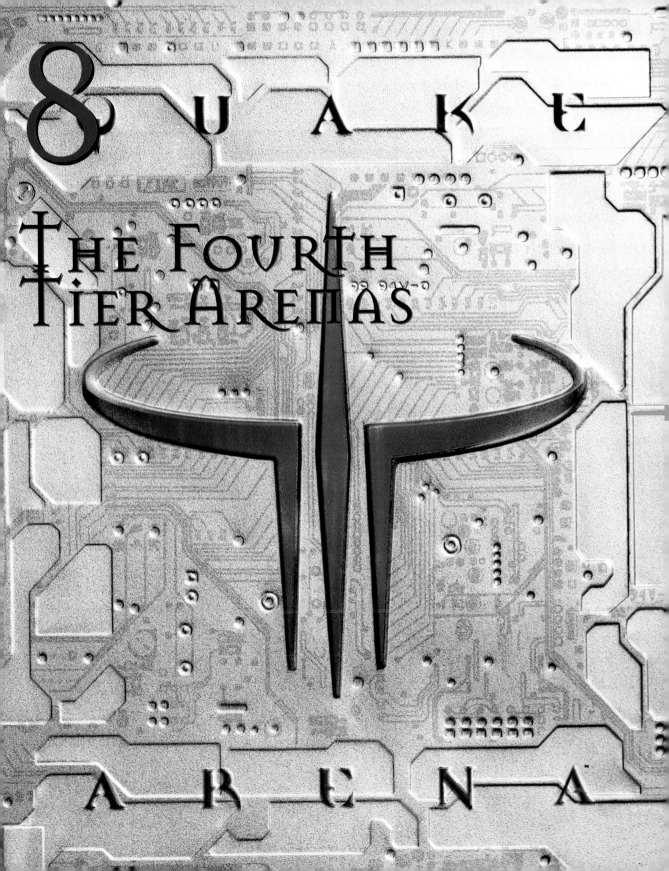

THE NAMELESS PLACE

SINGLE-PLAYER ENEMIES: ANGEL, WRACK, TANKJR
WEAPONS: ROCKET LAUNCHER, LIGHTNING GUN, PLASMA GUN
POWER-UPS: INVISIBILITY, QUAD, REGENERATION
FRAG LIMIT: 20

1. The power tube is located under the walkway in this area.
2. The power-ups appear under the stairs in a small alcove.
3. Yellow armor is found in these locations.
4. The rocket launcher is here.
5. The lightning gun is here.
6. The red armor is in this corner.
7. The plasma gun is here.
8. There is a large cache of ammunition in this spot.

08-MAP1

This arena contains a power tube that replenishes your health and armor when you stand in it. There are also a number of complex twists and turns on this level, and the staircases lead to different and various locations. Interconnecting corridors, large caches of ammunition, and three power-ups mark this as a unique map filled with surprises.

The power tube dominates this level. The problem is that using it makes a lot of noise, broadcasting the fact that you are healing to everyone on the level. You generally don't have more than a few seconds to heal yourself, so make the most of the time that you do spend in this area.

Tip

Don't get greedy in the power tube. You don't regenerate as quickly as your enemies can strip away your health, and you are vulnerable from several directions here.

Straight up from the power tube is a suit of yellow armor and the rocket launcher. These two items, combined with the power tube, make this area a haven for combat.

Follow the low corridors away from the power tube to the alcove-filled area below the stairs. You can find several health items here, several boxes of ammunition, and the power-up location. All three power-ups appear in the same spot, each appearing roughly one-third of the time. Naturally, the Quad is the most useful and the most coveted, but the invisibility icon is useful in these twisting halls as well.

The power tube is hard to miss. When you are in the tube, your visibility is poor, and you're wide open to being hit from almost all sides.

Grab the armor and the rocket launcher. Don't linger here since enemies usually abound in the vicinity.

Despite the health and ammunition here, these back corridors are less frequently traveled. This makes them a great place to heal up and get the ammunition you need.

All three power-ups appear on this spot under the stairs.

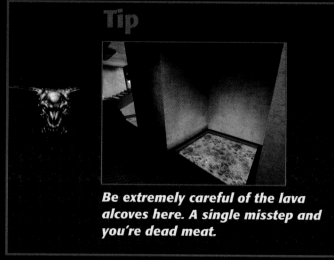

Tip

Be extremely careful of the lava alcoves here. A single misstep and you're dead meat.

Follow the staircases and catwalks up and around the level to find both the lightning gun and the plasma gun. Because this level tends to have very tight halls, the lightning gun is particularly useful. Opposite the lightning gun is a suit of red armor, which you should try to get as early as possible.

On the bridge above the power tube is a pair of gold healths. It's possible to rocket jump there, and the presence of the gold healths make it relatively painless.

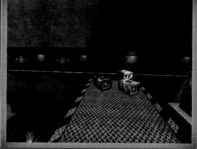

More useful weapons lie at the tops of the staircases. You can also find plenty of ammunition on the higher ground.

Gold health is another reason to spend some time on the higher ground.

Deva Station

SINGLE-PLAYER ENEMIES: LUCY, BIKER, PATRIOT, TANKJR
WEAPONS: SHOTGUN, GRENADE LAUNCHER, ROCKET LAUNCHER, LIGHTNING GUN, PLASMA GUN
POWER-UPS: PERSONAL TELEPORTER, MEDKIT, QUAD, HASTE
FRAG LIMIT: 20

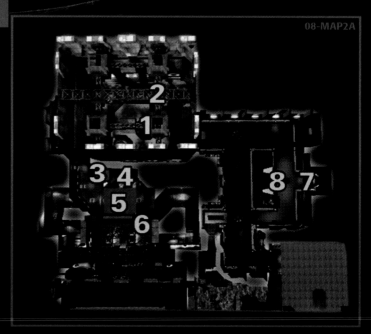

08-MAP2A

1. The rocket launcher is here.
2. There is a suit of red armor on this ledge.
3. A shotgun sits in this spot.
4. The medkit is here.
5. The first teleporter is located on the bottom floor under this ceiling.
6. The lightning gun is on a shelf here.
7. The second teleporter is here.
8. The secret compartment holding either gold health or the battle suit is across from the second teleporter.
9. There is yellow armor here.
10. The teleporter at number 7 brings you to this spot.
11. The plasma gun is behind a door here.
12. The Mega-Health is located directly over this bounce pad.
13. The haste power-up is here. You can open the door to the Quad room by shooting the target above the haste icon.
14. The Quad is here.
15. The teleporter at number 5 brings you here.

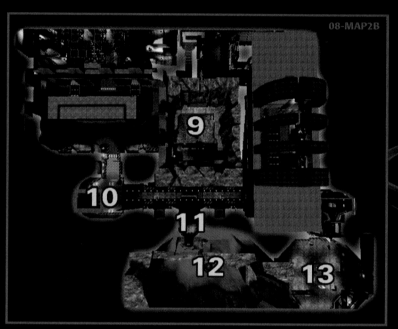

08-MAP2B

This is an extremely large map with a number of interesting secrets and surprises. Four power-ups appear scattered throughout this level, and all of the weapons except the railgun and the BFG10K are present as well. This level can be very confusing, but the hallways all interconnect with each other, and it's not too difficult to get from one place to the next.

In one corner of this map is the rocket launcher room. The rocket launcher is located on a platform surrounded by slime, so be careful when you get it. Jump off the bounce pad here to get to the ledge with red body armor and a gold health. There's also a pair of yellow healths and a trio of armor shards, as well as a box of rockets. From this room, you can exit into the main hallways on the ground floor or leave through the door at the top of the ramp.

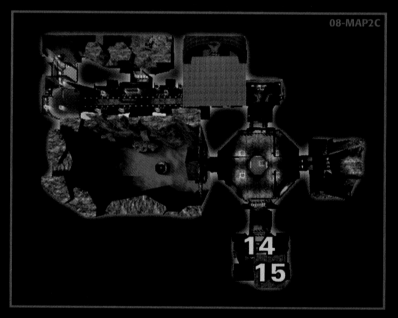

08-MAP2C

Through the door, you spot more ammunition and two more yellow healths, plus a shotgun in a small rounded alcove. Continue through the halls and near the cache of grenades and shells to grab the medkit. Go straight down the hall away from the medkit to the next area.

Follow the halls for one of the many shotguns in this arena, as well as the medkit.

The rocket launcher room contains a powerful weapon, ammunition, health, and armor. Therefore, it is heavily traveled and often battled over.

Here, you can find the lightning gun on one platform and a box of ammunition for it on another. The catwalks that lead away from these platforms both go to the same area, and they loop around to each other, making a large, irregular circle. Down both sides you find a pair of yellow healths and a shotgun, and the side with the ammunition holds an additional gold health. The real goal here is the teleporter in the middle.

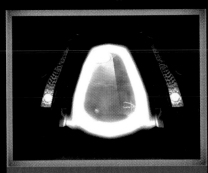

Follow the catwalk from the lightning gun to this teleporter.

Pop through the teleporter to appear in a small alcove containing health, ammunition, and the Quad. Getting the Quad is tricky, though, so be prepared to run. As soon as you grab it, the door to this room opens, and an array

The lightning gun is a great weapon for this level because of the many narrow corridors. A good shot is almost impossible to avoid.

of grenades begins to launch in the next room. Run up the stairs, straight through and nab the haste icon on the platform in the middle of this room. Then run straight ahead, back to the main hallways. The grenade launcher appears to your immediate right after the haste room.

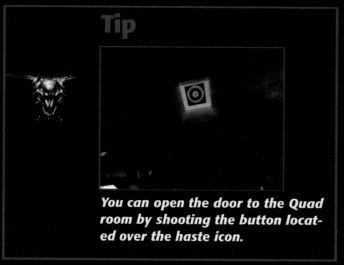

Tip

You can open the door to the Quad room by shooting the button located over the haste icon.

The corridor with the grenade launcher leads to a common melee spot on this level. There's another shotgun here, along with health. The alcoves along the sides of the walls are a perfect place to use for cover as you try to kill your enemies. Move through and turn right to another similar corridor. At the far end of this hallway, you spot a series of armor shards, as well as another shotgun. Going through the opening at the right leads back to the area with the lightning gun.

Nab the Quad, then run through the hail of grenades to score the haste power-up. This is an extremely powerful combination, so don't wait around—head to the busier areas of the arena and start shooting.

From the grenade launcher, follow the halls to this area filled with alcoves. Use these to avoid enemy fire. You must perfect your strafing technique to survive down here.

Midway down this corridor, there are a couple of turn-off points. The first is to the right. This access hallway contains a suit of yellow armor. You can run up the ramp to the higher level easily. Going here takes you to a very narrow set of stairs that leads back to the corridors outside the main floor level of the rocket launcher room.

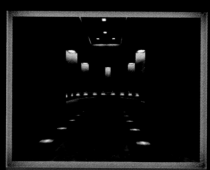

The armor shards in the back alcove are definitely worth grabbing.

Tip

You can rocket jump to the small transom over the entrance to this room. The slope in the ceiling helps guide you to the proper spot.

Across from the entrance to this access corridor, you find a door. Behind it is the plasma gun, an excellent weapon for the gunfighting areas here. Run through to the small balcony and jump out onto the bounce pad. Let the bounce pad take you straight up in the air to snag the Mega-Health. Jumping across to the other side brings you back to the haste room. Be extremely aware of the red fog that blankets the area around the bounce pad.

Not only can you score armor and ammunition, but you can also reach the main area quickly by using this corridor.

Tip

If you want a few seconds of real power, head through this side exit after getting the Quad and the haste power-up. You wind up with the plasma gun and about 20 seconds of both power-ups—a truly deadly combination.

The plasma gun is an excellent choice on this level, thanks to the number of walls and alcoves. It causes a lot of splash damage.

The Mega-Health is located near the top of the jump from the bounce pad. From it, you can easily make it to either ledge, but watch out for the fog of death.

The final major area is the set of corridors outside of the main floor of the rocket launcher room. These connect with the grenade launcher area, the access corridor, the rocket launcher room, and the lower gunfighting area. There are two notable locations here. The first is the teleporter, which is located straight away and right from the rocket launcher room. Get the shotgun in front of it and take the teleporter to the curved alcove filled with armor shards.

In single-player and deathmatch games, this battle suit is replaced by a gold health.

You can also open the wall immediately across from this teleporter. A secret alcove contains a gold health. However, in multiplayer team games, this gold health is replaced by a battle suit.

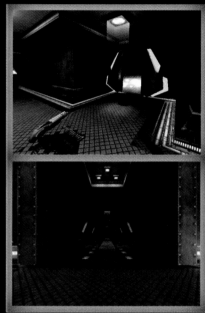

This teleporter leads you directly to the armor shards.

THE DREDWERKZ

SINGLE-PLAYER ENEMIES: SLASH, GORRE, LUCY, BIKER, PATRIOT, WRACK
WEAPONS: SHOTGUN, GRENADE LAUNCHER, ROCKET LAUNCHER, LIGHTNING GUN, RAILGUN, PLASMA GUN, BFG10K
POWER-UPS: QUAD, REGENERATION, PERSONAL TELEPORTER, MEGA-HEALTH
FRAG LIMIT: 20

1. The Quad appears here.
2. The Mega-Health is on a shelf here.
3. Plasma guns are located in these areas.
4. You will find the Regeneration icon in the water under this area.
5. The BFG can be found in a small room above the Regeneration icon. The teleporter in this room takes you to area number 6, and the teleporter at number 13 brings you here.
6. The teleporter in the BFG room takes you here, behind the yellow armor.
7. Yellow armor can be found here
8. Find the rocket launcher here.

08-MAP3A

9. The railguns are here.
10. Find the Personal Teleporter on the shelf below the plasma gun.
11. There is a lightning gun in this area.
12. Use the acceleration pads to reach the red armor over the canyon.
13. The teleporter here takes you to the BFG room.
14. The grenade launcher is in this area.

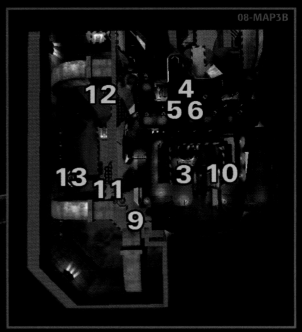

08-MAP3B

The Dredwerkz looks a lot more complicated than it really is, mostly because of the central courtyard area, which contains about 10 distinct ways to enter and leave. Everything in this Arena begins and ends with the central courtyard, and everyone is generally running to or from it, only to loop back to it again. Most of the action takes place here, simply because all roads lead to it.

Tip

This arena contains three levels of corridors. You can get a general idea of where you are by the shape of the hallways. The service corridors on the top level are narrow and dark. The middle level corridors tend to have curved, shiny walls. The lowest level passages are dim, and the walls are the same shape as the doorways. In the bottom two levels, the lighting tells you which side of the map you are on. The more brightly lit halls open into the courtyard across from the Quad, while the darker halls enter the courtyard on the same side as the Quad.

The two most obvious features of the courtyard area are both on the ground floor. First is the Quad, which is another reason the action tends to center around the courtyard area. The other obvious feature is the rectangular pool in the center of the room. Because the pool leads to several good weapons and power-ups, it almost always has a body in it somewhere.

The Quad tends to be a major focus of this level. You can generally find several enemies hovering around it.

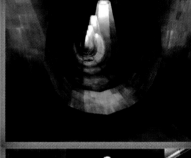

If you swim straight down in the pool and follow the tube, you run across the regeneration icon about halfway through. Swim straight up from here to reach the BFG room. Again, the fastest way out of this room is via the teleporter, which puts you back in the central courtyard, dumping you directly on top of the yellow armor across from the Mega-Health. Step out of this alcove/ledge to land on the rocket launcher.

Tip

This high ledge is an excellent sniping location since the only way to it is through the teleporter in the BFG room. You can score several quick kills by firing the BFG from here.

You can also swim through the pool all the way to the other side. Use the bounce pad to take you all the way up to the top level, where you land on a plasma gun. The two gold healths here are a welcome sight as well. Running out from the top level leads to a small hallway with a grenade launcher and two corridors. Taking the path to the right leads you back to the main courtyard

Swim through the lower tunnel and head up from the regeneration icon. You appear in the BFG room. The teleporter here takes you back to the main courtyard, armed with a very powerful weapon.

on a high ledge overlooking the pool. The Quad is on your right, and directly across from you is the suit of yellow armor you grabbed when you went through the teleporter in the BFG room.

If you don't take the turn-off back to the main court-yard, you can follow the hallway past a box of grenades and a box of rockets to the large open area on the side of the level. Like the courtyard, this area looks more confusing than it is, simply because you have a number of options here.

Perhaps the most obvious way to go is to drop off the edge to the right and down to the acceleration pad. Hit this to sail over the fog of death canyon into a suit of red armor. On the other side, you can grab a shotgun and take the bounce pad up to the second level or go

Use the bounce pad just off the pool in this room to reach the plasma gun on the top level.

through the door. The door leads to a short hallway with lightning gun ammunition and armor shards. This takes you back to the ground floor of the pool room you reached by swim-ming through the tunnel from the main courtyard.

This side courtyard area contains a number of important features and gives you a lot of options.

Here's another bird's-eye view of the main courtyard, this time from the other side.

The acceleration pads take you right into this suit of red armor.

Tip

This acceleration pad is hard to miss if you drop down here. However, it's difficult to get to the small ledge with the door on it.

If you take the bounce pad to the second level instead, you again have a couple of choices. Grab the railgun back and to the right of the bounce pad, then take a look around. There's a door on this level, which leads back to the middle level of the pool room with the plasma gun, an area we'll explore more fully in a moment. Continue on this level past the yellow armor to locate a bounce pad up to the top level where you entered.

On the far side of the acceleration pad jump, you can go back up to the next level or take the door. You can also take the acceleration pad back to the other side.

One again, you have a number of options here.

Your other option is to jump over to the platform sitting in the middle of the fog of death. There's nothing here but a teleporter, so walk through it. You appear in the BFG room, almost on top of the BFG itself. Grab it and get back to the central courtyard using the teleporter.

If you go through the door on the second level of this area instead, you enter the middle area of the room with the plasma gun, which you reached originally by swimming all the way through the tunnel from the main courtyard. Here, you can find a shotgun, some rockets, and some machine gun ammunition. Additionally, on a small ledge to the left you can find the personal teleporter. It's possible to rocket jump to it from here, but the easiest way to get it is to drop down from near the plasma gun.

The center of this room is rich with useful items.

Jump over to this teleporter to gain instant access to the BFG.

Also on this level, you see a pair of doors. Head through the door on the left to a circular area that leads back to the main courtyard. There's a Mega-Health on this shelf overlooking the pool and the Quad, making it well worth your while to go this way.

Take the door straight across from where you entered to find a whole new wing of this arena. You can grab some yellow armor just on the other side of the door. You're now on a balcony along the Quad side of the courtyard as you run down the path here. It ends in a door at the far side, which leads to a series of stairs and corridors, complete with a room holding a railgun.

Tip

As you near the door on the far side of this balcony, you can easily jump over to the platform holding the rocket launcher.

Exit the railgun room on the far side to find yet another chamber with two exits. You can head left, right, or straight from the gold health in front of you. Dropping off to the

The door on the left leads to an area overlooking the main courtyard, as well as an extremely valuable power-up.

left puts you right on top of a plasma gun, while heading straight also takes you to a drop to the lower area. Both of these ways through this room lead to a door that takes you to the ledge with the rocket launcher above the pool in the main courtyard.

This ledge runs along the side of the central corridor and gives you an excellent avenue to drop down to the Quad.

Go left or straight from the gold health to return to the courtyard.

If you head right from the gold health, you find the other side of the arena. Head down the stairs past some ammunition to a balcony above more red fog of death. By the yellow armor and the box of BFG ammunition, you can take the bridge to the door on the far side of this small canyon to get the grenade launcher next to the door. Drop down to the ground floor for the lightning gun, then follow the corridor through the door to find a shotgun, ammunition, and a passageway back to the ground level of the courtyard across from the Quad.

The grenade launcher waits by the top door while the lightning gun sits near the fog of death on the bottom.

All that remains of this level are the paths leading away from the door next to the grenade launcher over the lightning gun. If you go through this door, the rounded corridor takes you to a room with a pair of exits. Head down the stairs ahead of you to reach the small shelf with the acceleration pad. This pad takes you to the red armor in the open canyon on the side of the arena. If you go left through the door instead, you come to the courtyard, a short jump away from the rocket launcher. Take the stairs to the right for health and ammunition, as well as a drop down to the main floor.

Running through the door by the lightning gun takes you back to the courtyard and gives you a great view of anyone going for the Quad.

Drop off the left near the gold health for this plasma gun. The door leads to the rocket launcher in the main area while around to the right on the floor, a bounce pad brings you back up to the gold health.

Going straight from your entry in this room takes you to the red armor jump while heading left through the door returns you to the main courtyard area.

VERTICAL VENGEANCE

SINGLE-PLAYER ENEMY: ANARKI
WEAPONS: SHOTGUN, ROCKET LAUNCHER, RAILGUN, PLASMA GUN
POWER-UPS: MEGA-HEALTH
FRAG LIMIT: 10

1. The railgun appears here.
2. Red armor is here.
3. The plasma gun is here.
4. Find green health on the bottom floor here.
5. The rocket launcher is here.
6. Find the Mega-Health here.
7. The shotgun is on the top floor here.

08-MAP4

As with all of the tournament maps, this one is quite small. It is shaped like a large U, with an internal section that contains some important items. Navigating this level is sometimes confusing, but with practice, it isn't too hard.

Both the interior core of this level and the exterior U contain three levels. The ground floor of the interior doesn't hold much, except for a couple of yellow healths and a dangerous pool of slime. There are three doors here leading to the outside area.

The bottom level of the interior holds only health.

Outside the doors on the bottom level, you find a number of things. There are bounce pads at each end of the U, both of which lead to the top level, and the bottom right corner of the U holds a bounce pad to the second level. Along the right side of the U, you can find a series of green healths in a narrow corridor, and in the bottom left corner, you can locate the plasma gun.

The exterior of the second floor holds the rocket launcher, armor shards, and a lot of health.

If you take the bounce pad up to the second level, you can find the rocket launcher, with a pair of yellow healths, along the right side of the level. Follow this ledge around the base of the U to a door to the interior area. Following the ledge all the way around to the left side takes you past some armor shards and a small shelf with the Mega-Health.

If you take the door to the interior, you almost walk directly onto an acceleration pad. There are a few yellow healths on this level, but the main feature is this pad, which shoots you up to the top level, directly onto the railgun.

On the top floor by the railgun, there are doors on either side leading back to the exterior of the level. The right side of the U

The ground floor of the exterior holds valuable health and the plasma gun.

The shotgun is very useful for the close ranges that frequently occur in this small arena.

Except for the yellow healths, the main feature of the middle floor of the interior is the acceleration pad up to the railgun.

leads only to plasma gun ammunition, but the door to the left side of the U takes you to a box of rockets and the shotgun.

The most useful area on the exterior of the top level is the base of the U. Here you find a box of railgun ammunition, as well as a suit of red armor located on a small shelf hanging off the interior portion. Jump over to the shelf to grab the red armor.

9UAKE

The Fifth Tier Arenas

ARENA

Lost World

SINGLE-PLAYER ENEMIES: VISOR, RAZOR, STRIPE
WEAPONS: SHOTGUN, GRENADE LAUNCHER, ROCKET LAUNCHER,
LIGHTNING GUN
POWER-UPS: QUAD, MEGA-HEALTH, MEDKIT
FRAG LIMIT: 20

1. The rocket launcher is on this central platform of the bridge.
2. The Quad is sitting in a small alcove below the bridge.
3. The Mega-Health is located in an alcove under this roof.
4. The medkit is here.
5. The grenade launcher is in a corner here.
6. The teleporter is on the lowest level near the lava in this courtyard.
7. The teleporter from number 6 takes you to the bottom floor here.
8. The red armor is located here.
9. The lightning gun is here.

09-MAP1

The first arena on the fifth tier is much smaller than those on the fourth tier. There are only a few critical areas on this map, and the map has an extremely linear feel to it. Many areas have only one way, forcing you and your opponents to travel in particular directions. Because of this, there are several important locations for those who like to camp out and snipe.

The largest and most important area on the map is the large courtyard featuring the rocket launcher. This is located on the center of a bridge suspended over a long drop into lava. There is a gold health next to the rocket launcher, making this a very popular location. Both of the paths off the bridge lead to the external areas of the map.

The rocket launcher platform is heavily traveled. Much of the combat takes place here and on the levels below.

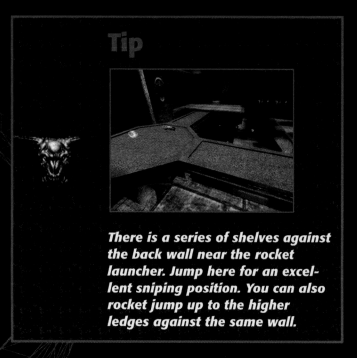

Tip

There is a series of shelves against the back wall near the rocket launcher. Jump here for an excellent sniping position. You can also rocket jump up to the higher ledges against the same wall.

Get the rocket launcher, then drop down to the Quad for a powerful combination.

The Quad appears in an alcove on the wall in this area. The easiest way to reach it is to drop down from the rocket launcher bridge. This is a decent spot to snipe from, but you are vulnerable because you don't have much room to move.

The next layer down, which is on approximately the same level as the Quad alcove, has three distinct paths off of it. With your back to the Quad, you can go right, left, or straight ahead. The right and central paths loop around to each other, meeting in the large room with the stitched wound on the ceiling. The green health here is a welcome sight, as is the yellow armor just outside this room.

Two of the paths from the platform under the rocket launcher lead to the yellow armor and the green health. Notice the Mega-Health on the platform behind the yellow armor.

There's also a small path near the wound room with a shotgun, some armor shards, and an angled bounce pad. This pad shoots you up to the top level, just to the right of the spot where you can drop down onto the Mega-Health. Following the corridor left takes you to the rocket launcher.

Tip

Drop down here to reach the Mega-Health without rocket jumping.

You also see the Mega-Health here. You can rocket jump to it, but it's better to drop down from the top level near the yellow health.

This angled bounce pad shoots you up to the top floor of the arena.

Your third choice standing in front of the Quad is to go left. If you go this way, you can find a couple of important exterior areas of this map. Head up the stairs past the flesh column to find the lightning gun. If you drop off to the right from here, you wind up back by the bottom of the flesh column. Go left for some new areas.

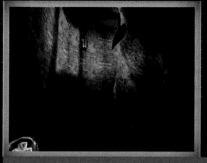

Run up the stairs by the flesh column and get the lightning gun at the top. Drop off to the right from the lightning gun and return back to the flesh column.

Tip

You can run around either side of the flesh column. Heading around it off the stairs can be a little quicker and can surprise an enemy.

Turn to the right at the top of the stairs past the lightning gun; this leads you back to the rocket launcher. Go left from here to get to the next important area. Running down the short set of stairs leads back to the rocket launcher area on the second level from the top. Stay near the top and head left to snag the grenade launcher and the medkit. If you drop all the way down, you're back in the wound room. Use the angled bounce pad here to get to the grenade launcher.

The grenade launcher is excellent when fired from the rocket launcher platform toward the lower areas in the same room. Don't pass up the medkit.

Drop through the small gap by the demon face to reach the red armor.

There's one other way off the second level in the rocket launcher courtyard. Drop down by the small demonic face to end up on the next platform down. This contains only the red armor and a box of rockets. There's no other way off this but to drop all the way down to the bottom level. Be careful of the lava.

Running through the teleporter on the bottom level of the rocket launcher room takes you back to the wound room facing the bounce pad.

On this bottom level, you can grab another shotgun and a gold health. The only way off this low level is to run through the teleporter, which places you back in the wound room.

Tip

The spot in the wound room facing where you teleport in is another excellent place to camp out. People frequently enter here and are slightly disoriented when they appear.

Grim Dungeons

SINGLE-PLAYER ENEMIES: VISOR, RAZOR, KEEL, STRIPE
WEAPONS: SHOTGUN, ROCKET LAUNCHER, LIGHTNING GUN, RAILGUN, PLASMA GUN, BFG10K
POWER-UPS: MEGA-HEALTH, PERSONAL TELEPORTER, QUAD
FRAG LIMIT: 20

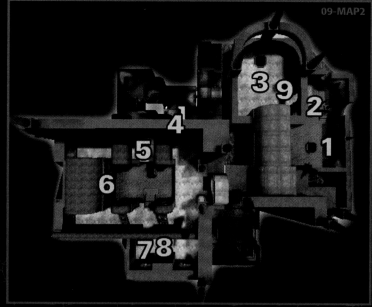

09-MAP2

1. The plasma gun is located just behind the drop to the catacombs.
2. The red armor is on a shelf up these stairs.
3. The Quad appears here.
4. The railgun is located on a platform below the floor here.
5. There's a suit of yellow armor here.
6. The rocket launcher is in this courtyard.
7. The personal teleporter is here.
8. The BFG10K waits through the gap here.
9. The lightning gun is in the catacombs under the floor here.

This arena holds two large courtyard areas and an extensive series of dangerous catacombs in the basement. While most of these low areas are covered, there are some spots where you can slip and fall into the fog of death. This level can get confusing, because most areas have several different possible paths out, including a trio of bounce pads in the catacombs.

The plasma gun courtyard is the most important area on the level. It holds a set of stairs down, a drop straight down into the basement area, and a short flight of stairs up. Take the stairs up and nab three types of ammunition, as well as a suit of red body armor. Grab this and run through the portal into the next courtyard area.

Tip

To drop down the holes without hitting the bounce pads at the bottom, run toward the higher-edged side of the hole and use air control to move yourself forward. Otherwise, you'll bounce right back up to the top.

The drop down in front of the plasma gun leads down to the catacombs level.

This area holds the Quad, as well as some ammunition. There's another hole in the floor here leading to the catacombs, and a long corridor with a door at the end. Follow this corridor for some plasma ammunition, then go through the door to find another corridor and a room with two gold healths, armor shards, a shotgun, and more ammunition. Both of the two doors out of this room lead to the second major area, the rocket launcher courtyard.

Grab the red armor in the alcove up the stairs from the plasma gun. The door here leads to the Quad area.

Move quickly to grab the Quad. Enemies are likely to hop up from the catacombs and snag it

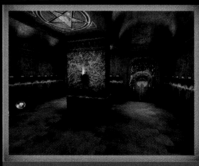

The door here, as well as the one on its left, leads into the rocket launcher courtyard.

Heading through the left door puts you on a line to grab the personal teleporter. There's a small rectangular drop-off to the left, which leads down into the basement area. Going through the right door leads into the main courtyard area, containing health and ammunition. The rocket launcher sits on the far side of the courtyard's outer rim, away from this entrance. To the right, there is some BFG ammunition and yellow armor. Notice another rectangular drop-off behind the BFG ammo. In addition, the courtyard has a lower level down a flight of stairs. This area contains yet another hole in the floor, which drops to the catacombs.

You can also leave this area via the door behind the yellow armor. This leads to a small drop-off with a bounce pad. Drop and turn right to find the railgun overlooking a low catacombs area containing the BFG. This is an excellent sniping

The gap next to the personal teleporter leads to the BFG area.

The rocket launcher is located on the other side of the courtyard behind the low wall.

position, because it contains two separate drops from the top level and is frequently traversed. Heading straight from this bounce pad takes you to the top layer of the catacombs.

Tip

Use the pillars in this area to hide behind when gunfighting with an enemy.

Now let's cover some of those drops from the top level. The simplest is the one located behind the BFG ammunition in the rocket launcher courtyard. Drop here to land on top of the Mega-Health. The Mega-Health can also be reached from the lower area of this courtyard, but it is in a long and narrow alcove, leaving you very vulnerable to attacks.

This railgun platform offers an excellent vantage point for the two main areas of the BFG room.

Getting the Mega-Health leaves you vulnerable to attacks from behind. This is why dropping in from above is the better way.

Drop through the circular hole at the bottom of the rocket launcher courtyard and you appear in the catacombs. A long chasm filled with the fog of death separates you from the BFG. On your side, you have yellow health, yellow armor, and rockets. This is a good position for sniping on the BFG area because you are protected from the railgun platform above.

Besides the bounce pad, there are two other ways to get to the BFG. You can jump onto the slow-moving platform that travels between you and the BFG. However, this leaves you very vulnerable because you have nowhere to go without falling into the fog of death. You can also head up the corridor to the left of where you entered this area.

The only way to the BFG from here is via the platform. The fastest way is to jump when you are about halfway across.

If you want to come down on the BFG side, drop through the small rectangular hole by the personal teleporter on the top level. You take some damage from the fall, but the gold health here helps alleviate this. Drop down to the BFG and snatch it up. The only way off of this side is to use the slow-moving platform, which leaves you wide open to attacks from the railgun platform.

Drop down next to the personal teleporter to get the BFG quickly. Keep in mind that you are exposed to the railgun platform here.

Heading away from where you dropped down from the rocket launcher courtyard, you enter the corridor area of the catacombs. After a few twists and turns, you have a choice of going either left or straight ahead. Going straight takes you directly to a bounce pad that leads back up to the plasma gun courtyard, the first hole in the floor that you encountered.

Should you head left, you enter a slightly more confusing area. This is a multilayered catacombs area, with armor and ammunition on the bottom floor. Head up the stairs, and on the middle level, locate the lightning gun near a bounce pad. This bounce pad rockets you up to the Quad area of the plasma gun courtyard. If you head all the way up the stairs and bear left, you enter the plasma gun courtyard. Heading right takes you over to the railgun platform.

The bounce pad in the distance leads back up to the plasma gun courtyard.

Run straight ahead to get the lightning gun, and use the bounce pad up to the Quad area. Running to the right takes you back to the plasma gun courtyard.

Health is the main reason to explore this area of the catacombs.

SINGLE-PLAYER ENEMIES: STRIPE, KEEL, RAZOR
WEAPONS: SHOTGUN, GRENADE LAUNCHER, ROCKET LAUNCHER, RAILGUN, PLASMA GUN, BFG10K
POWER-UPS: MEGA-HEALTH, TELEPORTER, QUAD, BATTLE SUIT
FRAG LIMIT: 15

1. The rocket launcher is in the center of this room.
2. The Mega-Health is near the ceiling under this domed roof.
3. Yellow armor is on the catwalk overlooking the rocket launcher.
4. The grenade launcher is here.
5. The Quad and the personal teleporter are in the basement under this area.
6. The battle suit appears here.
7. The railgun appears on this platform.
8. The BFG10K floats above the level here.
9. After getting the BFG10K, you land on the red armor here.
10. The secret area holding BFG10K ammunition is here.

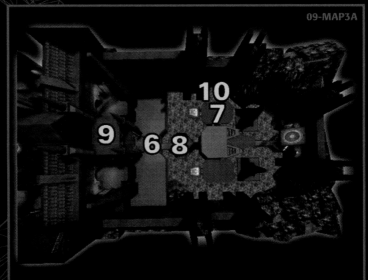

09-MAP3A

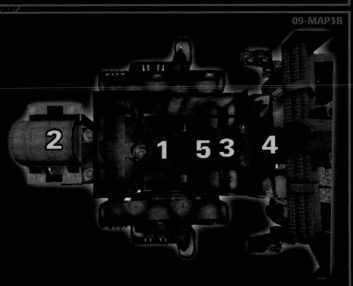

09-MAP3B

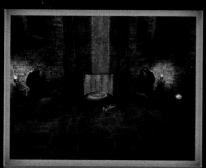

The rocket launcher room lies at the center of this level, and all roads lead to it eventually. It is the scene of much of your combat.

While the acceleration pads are faster, the bounce pad is protected from enemy fire.

Follow the yellow armor to the grenade launcher and some ledges overlooking the railgun area.

This level feels a lot larger than it really is, thanks in part to the huge, wide-open courtyard that contains both the railgun and the BFG. In addition to this significant area, the rocket launcher room is heavily traveled, as is the basement area containing both the Quad and the personal teleporter. It's impossible to get lost in the main areas of this level, but the side areas can be difficult to find if you don't know what to look for.

The rocket launcher room contains the most combat in this arena by far, due to its central location and the presence of the rocket launcher. There are a number of ways in and out of this room, which makes getting the rocket launcher somewhat difficult—you are often under fire from several different angles when you make a run for it.

The two acceleration pads and the bounce pad just behind the rocket launcher propel you up to the top ledge area. The two side passages up here lead around to the catwalk that overlooks the rocket launcher. Both of these side passages also contain a drop-off to a small set of staircases, which we'll discuss in a moment. At the yellow armor, you can run out and get the grenade launcher. Both of the paths from here lead to ledges overlooking the railgun courtyard. The right path also contains a yellow health.

If you take the bounce pad up from the rocket launcher, you see another path straight ahead of you. The Mega-Health is located above this narrow bridge, out of your reach. You can rocket jump up to it, or you can drop off either side onto the angled bounce pads, which launch you directly into the Mega-Health. Once you have it, use air control to land back on the bridge. The gap at the end of this bridge drops to a bounce pad in the basement area. You can also reach the bounce pads up to the Mega-Health by running through either of the two doorways next to the bounce pad. This way also gives you some additional rocket launcher and railgun ammunition and a gold health.

In the other direction from the rocket launcher, there are five distinct paths out of the area: one on each side, two doorways ahead to the left and right, and a gap in the floor straight ahead of you. Both the leftmost and rightmost passageways lead down into the basement. Go left to find two yellow healths, BFG ammunition, and a plasma gun. Go right to get yellow armor, machine gun and plasma gun ammunition, and a second plasma gun. These two side branches meet again at the bottom.

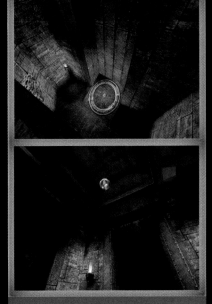

Tip

The gaps on the sides of either of the top catwalks drop into these two staircases. If you are on the top level, this is the quickest way to the basement.

Use the bounce pads on the floor below you to bounce up to the Mega-Health overhead.

In the basement, there are a couple more yellow healths and the personal teleporter. A long, narrow bridge also holds the Quad. This is an extremely dangerous area. On either side of the bridge, the red fog of death threatens you. Additionally, there are three huge inverted crosses swinging back and forth across the bridge. A hit from one of these kills instantly. If you do run all the way across, you can find armor shards, rockets, yellow health, and the shotgun. Directly behind the shotgun is a bounce pad that takes you back up to the Mega-Health area.

The area behind the rocket launcher is also filled with exits.

Tip

Grab the personal teleporter, run past the first two crosses, and use the personal teleporter to take you out of this area immediately.

Both of the side passages from behind the rocket launcher contain plasma guns.

The personal teleporter is extremely useful on this level, particularly in getting the Quad and getting back to the battle quickly. Be careful around the swinging crosses. One touch and you are done for.

Back at the rocket launcher, you still have three unexplored paths. The archways to the right and left of the drop-off both lead out to the railgun area. The battle suit appears right outside of the doorway into this area, and you can grab both yellow armor and a gold health off to the left. If you drop off the center of the ledge, you land on a low platform. Follow the corridor here for some armor shards and health. This small hallway ends in a bounce pad that pops you into the rocket launcher room again, through the central gap that you hadn't yet explored.

Should you make it across the bridge, you'll find several useful items. Directly across from the shotgun is a bounce pad to the Mega-Health area.

Instead of dropping straight down from the battle suit, you can also jump out onto the bounce pad. This sends you over to the far platform where the railgun awaits. The two acceleration pads hurl you back to the area with the grenade launcher. There are more interesting things to do here before jumping back, however.

The battle suit protects you if you fall into the lava. It's also incredibly useful for the rocket jumps you can make in this area.

Tip

The walls near the battle suit are filled with high, dark ledges that you can rocket jump to.

Tip

Notice that the area surrounding the railgun platform is filled with lava. If you fall into it, jump toward the central platform and get onto the low bridge.

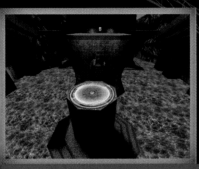

Bounce off this pad out to the railgun area. The acceleration pads send you back to the catwalk above the main area of the level.

From the center of this platform, look straight up. That thing floating up in the sky is the BFG. So how do you get it? Turn and look at the armor shards. There's a bounce pad floating above them. If you rocket jump from the middle shard and air control yourself onto this pad, it takes you directly into the BFG. You land on a small shelf overlooking this area directly on a suit of red body armor—quite a haul.

If you miss the jump, or don't want to try it, drop and follow the low bridge back to the rocket launcher room. Or, if you missed and wish to try again, use the teleporter, which takes you back to the area where the battle suit appears.

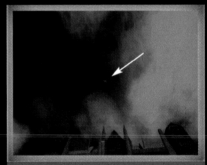

That's the BFG floating way up in the sky. Getting it takes a little work on your part.

Tip

If you just want the BFG and don't care about the red armor, you can rocket jump off the bounce pad leading to the railgun directly up to the BFG.

Tip

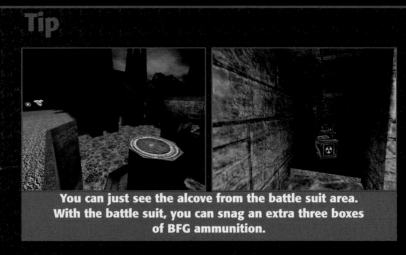

You can just see the alcove from the battle suit area. With the battle suit, you can snag an extra three boxes of BFG ammunition.

If you have the battle suit, you can score some extra BFG ammunition. Facing the lava, look left. Get the battle suit and run into the small alcove. There are three boxes of BFG ammunition here. The only way in and out of this area is through the lava, so without the battle suit, you can't survive. A quicker way out of this alcove is to use the personal teleporter once you grab the ammunition.

Rocket jump from the middle of the armor shards up to the bounce pad. This sends you on an arc into the BFG, ending on top of the red armor. Now merely drop back to the lower area and run to the rocket launcher room.

SINGLE-PLAYER ENEMIES: URIEL
WEAPONS: SHOTGUN, ROCKET LAUNCHER, PLASMA GUN
POWER-UPS: QUAD
FRAG LIMIT: 10

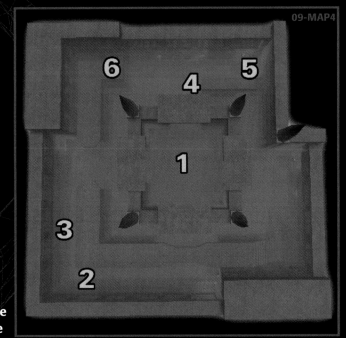

09-MAP4

1. The rocket launcher appears on the dais in the middle of the map.
2. The plasma gun is here.
3. There's a row of armor shards here.
4. The yellow armor is here.
5. The shotgun lies in this corner.
6. Run up the stairs and jump the gap to find the Quad in this spot.

This is a small arena, shaped like a box. For the most part, there is only one level here, although there is a staircase along the side of the map that leads up to the Quad. What makes this map difficult is that the entire level is shrouded by fog. You have very limited visibility, and shots often come out of the mists from unknown directions. While skill plays a major part in your success, there are some elements of luck involved on this map as well.

Tip

Since visibility is reduced on this map, rely more on your hearing. Walking instead of running not only allows you to hear your opponent more easily, it makes you quieter, allowing you to sneak up on an unsuspecting foe.

As already mentioned, this level is effectively a large square. At the center of this square is a large dais holding the rocket launcher at its center and a gold health off to one side. The rocket launcher, because of its splash damage, is highly desirable in this arena, and you can expect combat to center around it often.

If you wish to rise out of the mists, you can rocket jump to the tops of the arches surrounding the central platform. This can give you a better look at the map and the position of your enemy, but it also leaves you out in the open, making you an easier target.

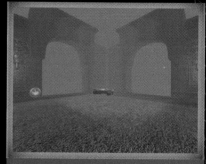

Combat often focuses on the rocket launcher in part because this area is visible from virtually everywhere on the map.

This bird's-eye view of the rocket launcher makes seeing your enemy easier, but it also exposes you to more fire.

The outer area of the level is set up like a spiral. From the rocket launcher, turn and locate the gold health in the exterior. Run to the back wall and turn right, following this narrow passage behind the obstruction to your right. You find the plasma gun back here. Around the next corner, you run across four armor shards.

The outer spiral starts behind the gold health and under the rockets on the top bridge.

The steady stream of fire from the plasma gun makes you more visible in the fog, but the damage it causes is worth it.

Listen for your opponent grabbing the armor shards. Because these are the only armor shards on the level, you'll hear know where he is when you hear the familiar sound.

Continue past the armor shards to the box of machine gun ammunition. Above this box on a high ledge is the Quad. Turn the corner again to find the yellow armor (another important sound cue). Head left past the armor to locate the shotgun in a back corner.

Past the next corner, you see a set of stairs rising out of the fog. There's a gold health on the first landing. Take the stairs to the top and run along this shelf. You can easily jump to the next shelf, where you can pick up some plasma cells and the Quad. Because this shelf takes you up out of the fog, you are more visible and can be targeted more easily.

Because of the close quarters, the shotgun often scores a quick kill.

Head up the stairs and around the ledge to the Quad. Like rocket jumping to the central arches, this takes you out of the fog, making you more easily spotted by your opponent.

Tip

For a sneakier way to nab the Quad, you can rocket jump to it easily.

Tip

The Quad is something of a mixed blessing on this map. While it increases the amount of damage you do, it also makes you much more visible to your enemy.

Note

The Quad appears much less frequently than you are used to. Expect to hear it reappear about half as often as on earlier levels.

IOuake

The Sixth Tier Arenas and The Final Level

ARENA

The Bouncy Map

SINGLE-PLAYER ENEMIES: CADAVRE, BONES, DOOM
WEAPONS: SHOTGUN, ROCKET LAUNCHER, RAILGUN, PLASMA GUN
POWER-UPS: NONE
FRAG LIMIT: 20

1. The railgun is on this top platform.
2. A suit of red armor sits here.
3. The plasma gun lies on a small shelf directly under the railgun.
4. The shotgun is located here.
5. The rocket launcher is in this location.
6. The yellow armor is on a low shelf here.

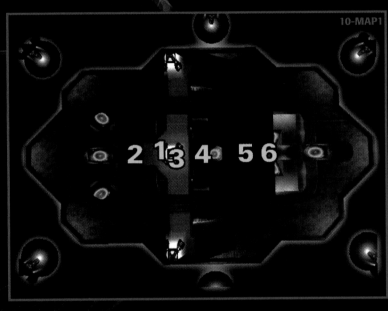

10-MAP1

This level gets its name from the huge number of bounce pads in it.
Because of all of these bounce pads, this arena tends to be fast and furious, with constant action. It's a difficult map to camp on, because almost anywhere is accessible from almost anywhere else in just a few seconds.

Tip

The edges of this map are particularly dangerous. While there is no fog of death, falling off the edge into space is just as fatal.

On the very top level of the arena, you find a platform holding the railgun. This is an excellent vantage point, offering a view of two frequently traveled areas, but you are also extremely exposed in this location. There are two sets of stairs leading up to the railgun, and the lack of health and armor makes it a difficult position to hold.

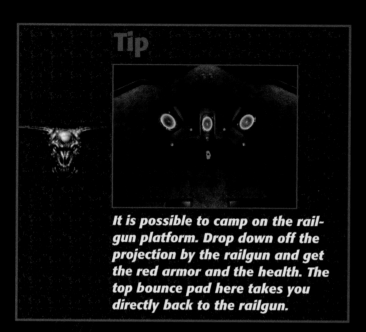

Tip

It is possible to camp on the railgun platform. Drop down off the projection by the railgun and get the red armor and the health. The top bounce pad here takes you directly back to the railgun.

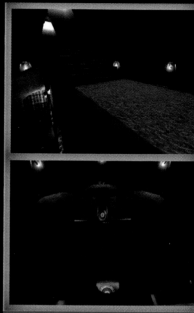

The railgun platform isn't easy to hold for long, but you should have enough time to get off a couple of quality shots.

On the front side of the level, straight down from the projection on the railgun platform, you find the plasma gun. You can drop all the way down to the basement area from here or down to the next lower level, which holds the red armor. If you drop to the plasma gun, explore this area to find two armor shards and a shotgun.

The plasma gun and the red body armor should be welcome additions.

Below the red armor is a pair of ledges containing two yellow healths each. The two bounce pads in the corners pop you back to the plasma gun area, while the bounce pad against the back wall sends you all the way back to the railgun. The railgun ammunition is particularly useful if you are going to hop back up to the top.

On the other side of the level, behind the railgun platform, you see the ledge holding the rocket launcher. There's some additional rocket launcher ammunition on the far side. Dropping to the area behind you, back toward the railgun platform, takes you to the shotgun. Drop toward the edge of the map to find a suit of yellow armor. The two angled bounce pads by the shotgun hop you back to the rocket launcher.

Again, there are three bounce pads on the edge of the map. The two side bounce pads each have a gold health on top of them, and both take you to the sides of the catwalk surrounding this area. The bounce pad on the edge of the map pops you onto the rocket launcher.

The central area of the basement holds several pairs of yellow health, as well as boxes of shotgun and machine gun ammunition. The single horizontal bounce pad here shoots you onto the shotgun.

The middle bounce pad here launches you all the way back to the top of the map. If you don't use air control, you'll land right on top of the railgun.

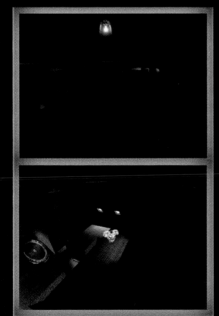

The rocket launcher and the yellow armor are both useful here. Aside from the railgun, the rocket launcher is the most sought-after weapon on this level.

The basement area is often action-packed, simply because most of the respawning areas are here. Machine gun duels are frequent events.

The Longest Yard

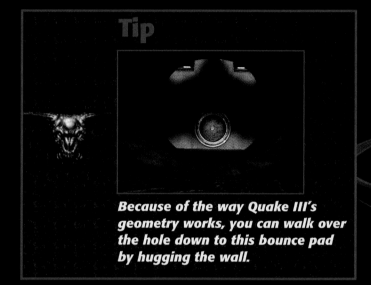

Tip

Because of the way Quake III's geometry works, you can walk over the hole down to this bounce pad by hugging the wall.

SINGLE-PLAYER ENEMIES: MAJOR, SORLAG, DOOM
WEAPONS: SHOTGUN, ROCKET LAUNCHER, RAILGUN
POWER-UPS: QUAD, MEGA-HEALTH
FRAG LIMIT: 20

1. The Mega-Health is located directly above this central bounce pad.
2. This bounce pad leads to the Quad.
3. The Quad is located here.
4. The three teleporters all take you to number 5.
5. The red armor sits on this bridge.
6. Rocket launchers are in these locations.
7. Shotguns are located in these areas.
8. The railgun is here.

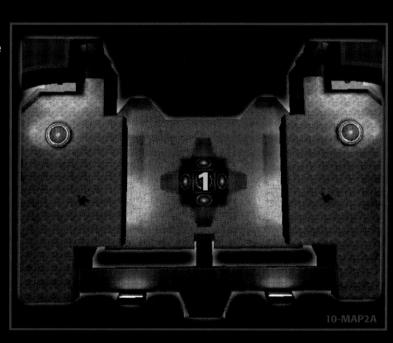

10-MAP2A

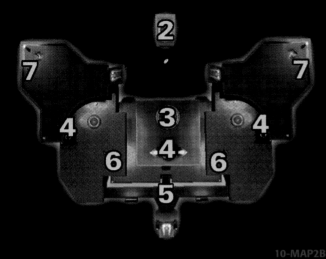

10-MAP2B

Like the first arena in this tier, this map is surrounded by space, and the map's edges are easily walked over if you aren't careful. This is a fast and furious level, with powerful weaponry condensed into a relatively small area. The large number of bounce pads means a lot of bodies flying around constantly, which makes for difficult shots with the rocket launcher. However, this is a railgun expert's dream level.

This arena has a main area with three floors, a small top platform, and a distant area containing the railgun. Most of the action takes place in the central area because the railgun can be difficult to get. The bottom floor of the arena contains a central structure with an angled bounce pad on each side. Three of these bounce pads send you up to the second level while the fourth launches you much higher. We'll come back to this bounce pad in a second.

10-MAP2C

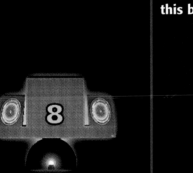

This bounce pad box is the only way from the bottom level up to the next higher set of platforms. Off to the right, you can see the path to the railgun. The bounce pad on the left leads up to the Quad.

The central structure also has a bounce pad on the top. If you jump onto this from the second level of the main section, it launches you straight into the air, where you can snag the Mega-Health. Once you have this, you can easily use air control to reach one of the side platforms.

The bottom area of the map also contains gold healths in the corners. These are naturally very valuable, but they are difficult to get safely. Even an indirect rocket hit can knock you off the platform and into outer space. There's also a pair of railgun ammo boxes and an acceleration pad. Take the pad to reach the railgun platform.

The top of the bounce pad box leads to this Mega-Health. However, a railgun expert can pick you off easily, making getting the Mega-Health almost moot.

Tip

Watch for people following you on the acceleration pad. If you are skilled with the railgun, you can pick them off as they fly in.

The acceleration pad shoots you over to the railgun platform.

The railgun platform has only a few features besides the railgun itself. On either side, there is a yellow health and an angled bounce pad that launches you onto the main area of the level. This can be a difficult spot to guard, especially if someone else has already grabbed a railgun and bounced back. However, you should be able to score a couple of kills from here before launching yourself into the main area.

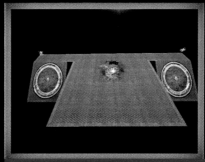

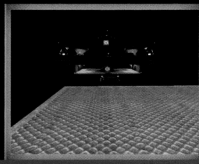

You should have enough time to get off a shot or two before the others figure out where you are and retaliate.

Up from the bottom level of the main area are two side ledges with several features. Both hold a rocket launcher and ammunition. Both also have bounce pads to the top level. Additionally, on each of these ledges there's a teleporter. Use this to get to the center of the bridge connecting these ledges. The red armor appears here periodically.

Tip

Going through the teleporter makes you a sitting duck for the railgun, especially if someone is firing from the railgun platform.

Using either of the bounce pads launches you up to the top level of the main area. Each of these platforms holds a gold health, some ammunition, and a shotgun. The acceleration pads on each side launch you to the top platform across the way, and the armor shards and yellow armor you grab en route will help you survive.

The central platforms are heavily trafficked. You spend a lot of time here fighting over rocket launchers.

The teleporters here put you directly on top of the red armor.

Tip

The shotgun is a good choice if you are coming from the acceleration pad, and another player is on the opposite platform. You can also air control yourself to land directly on the opposite pad, allowing you to get in a few shots before hopping back.

But what about the Quad? Remember that fourth bounce pad on the bottom level of the map? Landing on it launches you into a second, higher bounce pad—no air control needed. You bounce off of this pad

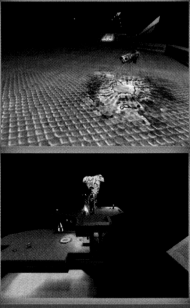

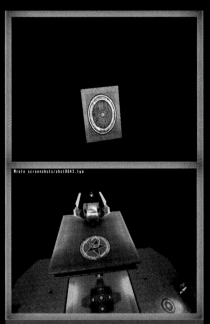

directly onto the Quad on the tiny platform situated high above the level. You can drop down off of this platform, but this causes significant damage. You can also run through the teleporter, which puts you onto the middle of the bridge on the central level, right where the red armor appears.

The main feature on the top floor of the main area is the acceleration pad jump to the yellow armor.

Bounce off the pad opposite the railgun acceleration pad and up to the higher bounce pad just past the yellow armor. This sends you up even higher to the Quad platform. The teleporter here plants you on the red armor.

Tip

Like going through a teleporter, grabbing the Quad leaves you open to railgun attacks. Furthermore, since getting it requires two bounce pad jumps and a teleport to the red armor, anyone with a railgun gets three quality shots at you before you can start dealing damage.

Tip

If you hear someone pick up the Quad and you have a railgun, equip it and aim at the red armor. As soon as the enemy appears, fire.

SPACE CHAMBER

SINGLE-PLAYER ENEMIES: CADAVRE, BONES, MAJOR, KEEL, SORLAG
WEAPONS: SHOTGUN, ROCKET LAUNCHER, RAILGUN
POWER-UPS: QUAD, PERSONAL TELEPORTER
FRAG LIMIT: 20

1. Rocket launchers are situated between the acceleration pads.
2. The railgun is on this exposed platform.
3. The personal teleporter is here.
4. The Quad can be found at the top of the jump from the bounce pad here.
5. Red armor is located on small shelves under this area.
6. Shotguns are found here.

If you aren't enjoying the levels that take place in outer space, you're going to have a real problem with this map. It is dominated by huge open staircases with drops off the side into nothingness. The level is symmetrical, with two separate acceleration pads/rocket launcher jumps, shotgun and green health groups, and red armor platforms. This is an extremely vertical level, and you draw fire from all angles as you run through it.

Starting at the back side in the center, you spot the personal teleporter. This is perhaps the most important item to possess on this level, even more so than the Quad. Since a single misstep can send you off into the void, this item acts as an insurance policy. Around either side from the personal teleporter are gold health crosses. You can either take the passageways to the sides of the map or drop to the lower area in the middle. Both sides of this drop contain bounce pads leading back up to the personal teleporter.

The personal teleporter can save you from an ignoble death should you fall off the edge of this dangerous arena.

Yellow armor and yellow health can be found through the middle of the level at the bottom.

Running straight through the center of the map on the lowest level is a narrow corridor holding a suit of yellow armor and a pair of yellow healths. Off each side from the yellow armor is a bounce pad that launches you to the bridge overhead. The railgun is here, with staircases leading off to both sides.

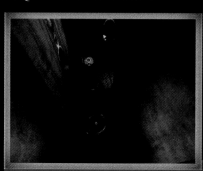

The bounce pads located under the personal teleporter bring you back to the top level.

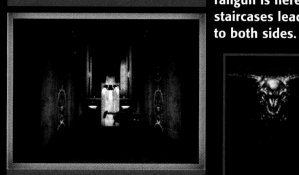

The railgun is a powerful weapon on this level, but its platform is difficult to defend.

Tip

It's tempting to stand on the railgun platform and take potshots at passing enemies. However, because this level is so open, and because of the railgun's central location, this is a very dangerous place to stand.

Behind the railgun, or straight ahead from the yellow armor, there is another bounce pad. Taking this sends you straight up into the sky, where you grab a trio of green healths. At the top of your bounce, you also encounter the Quad. From here, you can easily air control yourself over to one of the nearby ledges.

Tip

Getting the Quad is dangerous because the bounce pad leaves you vulnerable to anyone standing on the railgun platform. A better way to get the Quad is to rocket jump from one of the higher areas near the Quad, because this leaves you much less vulnerable to sniping.

Getting the Quad leaves you vulnerable to snipers, but if you manage to grab it, you can have a field day with the rocket launchers.

The two sides of the map going out from the center are mirror images of each other. From the top level, near the Quad, run over to find a gold health and an acceleration pad. This pad launches you across the level, giving you a rocket launcher on the way. Running through the exit on the far side takes you back to the personal teleporter. You can also go down the stairs on the side with the gold health.

Down the first flight of stairs, turn toward the center of the level to find the railgun platform straight ahead. Head down two more flights of stairs for more possibilities. The bounce pad just off the third set of stairs takes you straight up, giving you the rocket launcher located between the acceleration pads.

Head down one flight of stairs and up the next to grab the railgun.

Straight ahead from these stairs is a small series of platforms with a suit of red armor and a box of rockets at the end. It looks at first like you have to jump from platform to platform, but you can simply run across to get the armor. The problem here is that these small platforms are surrounded by space, so even a minor hit from an enemy can send you flying to your death.

Hit the acceleration pad to jet over to the other side and score the rocket launcher.

The red armor looks tempting, but that first step off the side is fatal.

Tip

Grab the red armor and fall off the far side of the platform. There's a bounce pad here that launches you all the way to the top of the level, near the rocket launcher acceleration pad.

If you run toward the middle from the bottom of the third set of stairs, you head straight across the center near the yellow armor. Two bounce pads against the back wall launch you up onto the gold health icons next to the personal teleporter.

Your final option from this set of stairs is to continue all the way to the bottom level. A small area here contains a shotgun surrounded by four green healths. Run up the opposite set of stairs and then toward the center of the map to find the bounce pad leading up to the Quad.

Because of the many tight staircases and narrow passages through the center of the level, the shotgun is extremely powerful.

This bounce pad pops you to the top level near the personal teleporter.

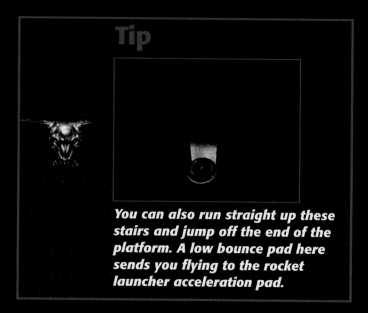

Tip

You can also run straight up these stairs and jump off the end of the platform. A low bounce pad here sends you flying to the rocket launcher acceleration pad.

APOCALYPSE VOID

SINGLE-PLAYER ENEMIES: CADAVRE, DOOM, SORLAG
WEAPONS: SHOTGUN, ROCKET LAUNCHER, RAILGUN, PLASMA GUN
POWER-UPS: QUAD, FLIGHT (MULTIPLAYER ONLY)
FRAG LIMIT: 20

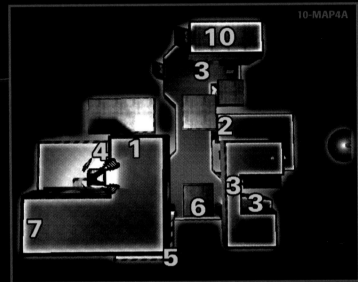

10-MAP4A

1. The railgun is located on this high ledge.
2. Find the plasma gun on this shelf.
3. Shotguns are found in these three areas.
4. Yellow armor is in these locations.
5. There is a rocket launcher here.
6. In multiplayer games, the flight icon appears on the bottom floor under this elevator platform.
7. The personal teleporter is one floor down under this area.
8. The rocket launcher on the far platform is here.
9. The Quad appears here.
10. Red armor is here.

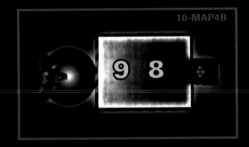

10-MAP4B

This level looks quite confusing. The huge number of moving elevator platforms makes it difficult to get a good sense of where everything is. However, the level itself is really quite simple. There is a main area with a series of platforms suspended in space. Off in the distance is another platform reachable by a pair of acceleration pads. The elevators serve as the only means to get from the lower floors to the higher platforms, which are much more beneficial in terms of items, weapons, and ammunition.

The lowest floor is surprisingly bare. There are two gold healths here, as well as a pair of shotguns. On one side is an acceleration pad leading over to the distant ledge.

Otherwise, this is simply a wide-open space with little cover. Take one of the three elevators off of this level as soon as you can.

The lowest floor of this level is barren and open.

In multiplayer games, the flight power-up also appears on the bottom level.

The next level up contains a single platform at the back of the map. You can grab the plasma gun here, as well as some cells. A suit of yellow armor sits on this platform in the back corner.

There are several platforms the next floor up. Just above the platform with the yellow armor is a higher area containing another shotgun, some ammunition, and a gold health. Across the way, reachable by elevator platform, is a second shelf. This one also holds a gold health, as well as a suit of red armor. The acceleration pad here is directly above the one on the lowest floor, and like the lower one, it leads to the distant ledge.

Because of the open nature of this level, you must be accurate to use the plasma gun effectively.

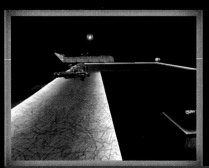

The middle levels contain several useful items. The acceleration pad launches you through space to the distant Quad platform.

Slightly higher than these two floors, toward the middle of the map, is a question mark-shaped floor holding a number of important items. A rocket launcher, yellow armor, gold health, two boxes of rockets, and a box each of cells and slugs can be grabbed here. Most importantly, the personal teleporter is located on this floor as well. As in the previous levels of this tier, the personal teleporter is an excellent insurance policy should you fall off the side.

The highest area is an L-shaped platform holding the railgun. There are four elevators that lead all the way to this area, three on one side and one in the back. As the highest point on the map, this is an excellent location for sniping with the railgun. It is, however, exposed, and the lack of health and other defensive items makes it a vulnerable location.

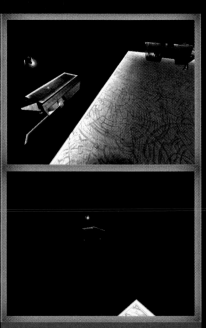

Both the rocket launcher and the personal teleporter are critical. The rocket launcher is excellent from the higher ground, thanks to the splash damage it creates, while the personal teleporter can bring you back if you fall off the sides.

The railgun platform is a great sniping location, but it is extremely exposed and vulnerable.

Tip

The railgun appears near where the three elevators rise to this level. The best sniping location is on the other end of the platform, because it gives you an unobstructed view of the Quad area. However, if you camp here, you are easy pickings for anyone else coming up to this high ledge.

Both acceleration pads on the lower floors send you across the void to a small area. The two yellow healths, rocket launcher, and rockets are a nice find, but the real prize here is the Quad. However, since the jump to this platform is long, you are vulnerable to railgun hits. The platform itself is extremely open to railgun shots from virtually everywhere on the map. The acceleration pad here launches you back toward the main level. You land near the higher acceleration pad on the middle floor.

The Quad is difficult to use from this platform because of the close quarters. Take the acceleration pad back to the main area and deal damage from there.

The Very End
of You

SINGLE-PLAYER ENEMY: XAERO
WEAPONS: SHOTGUN, ROCKET LAUNCHER, RAILGUN, BFG10K
POWER-UPS: PERSONAL TELEPORTER, MEGA-HEALTH
FRAG LIMIT: 10

1. Rocket launchers are positioned here.
2. Find railguns between these pillars.
3. Both the personal teleporter and red armor appear between the acceleration pads.
4. The BFG10K rests on this platform overlooking the rest of the map.
5. The Mega-Health appears here.
6. This teleporter takes you to one of four random locations on the level.

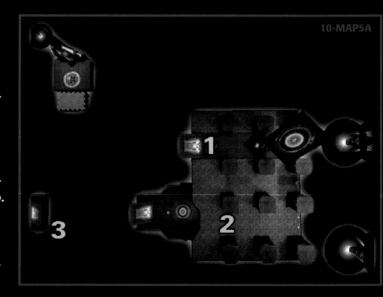

7. Shoot this button to drop the ceiling of the BFG platform. This crushes anything on it.

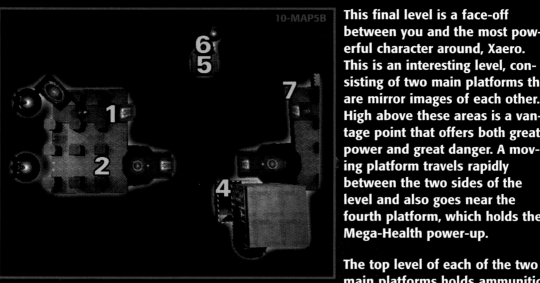

10-MAP5B

This final level is a face-off between you and the most powerful character around, Xaero. This is an interesting level, consisting of two main platforms that are mirror images of each other. High above these areas is a vantage point that offers both great power and great danger. A moving platform travels rapidly between the two sides of the level and also goes near the fourth platform, which holds the Mega-Health power-up.

The top level of each of the two main platforms holds ammunition for all of the weapons in this arena, as well as gold health, a rocket launcher, and a railgun. The rocket launcher is situated right in front of the acceleration pad, while the railgun sits near the drop down to the small shelf resting below the top level.

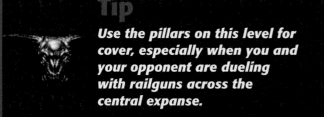

Tip

Use the pillars on this level for cover, especially when you and your opponent are dueling with railguns across the central expanse.

The rocket launcher is useful for raining death on a close enemy while the railgun is perfect for shots across the central void.

Tip

It's also no problem to rocket jump to the top of these pillars.

Dropping by the railgun reveals three important items. The first is the bounce pad, which sends you back up to the railgun area. The second is another gold health. The third is the acceleration pad that launches you to the same low shelf on the other side of the map.

This acceleration pad jump is important not only because it is the best and fastest way between the two sides of the level, but also because you can grab either the personal teleporter or the red armor as you go across. These two items appear at approximately the midpoint of this trip, each showing up about half the time.

The lower platforms hold the fastest and best way to cross over the central void.

Using the moving platform leaves you exposed to railgun shots, but it's the only way to get the Mega-Health.

The moving platform travels next to the acceleration pads on the top level of the map. Stepping onto this platform can be difficult because of its speed, but this is the only way to reach the small ledge in the middle of space. Here you can grab the Mega-Health. The teleporter is the quickest way off this ledge. It acts much like the personal teleporter, taking you to one of four random locations around the map.

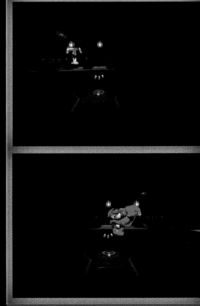

Both the personal teleporter and the red body armor appear on the jump between the two main platforms.

This teleporter takes you to one of four random locations elsewhere on the level.

The acceleration pads just behind the rocket launchers are unique on this map. Rather than sending you across to the other side, they send you flying into one of the bounce pads angled above the main map area. Bouncing off one of these takes you to the platform that towers over the level. You can find both yellow health and the BFG10K here.

The real prize is the BFG10K on this platform. Don't stay here long or you'll be crushed by the ceiling.

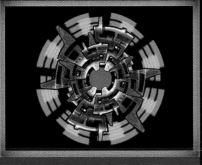

This target controls the ceiling on the BFG platform.

However, this platform is not without its dangers. The small red sphere near it, when shot, causes the ceiling to collapse, instantly crushing anything under it. If there is something on the platform when the ceiling is brought down, it immediately springs back open. If nothing rests on the platform, it remains closed for about three seconds.

When the sphere is activated, the BFG platform is unreachable for a few seconds

Tip

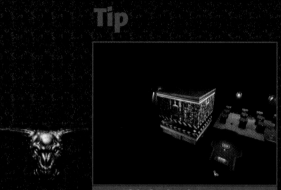

This looks dangerous, but with proper timing, the ceiling will raise up before you reach the platform. You have exactly half a second to get the BFG and jump off to the main area before the ceiling can be activated.

The crushing ceiling opens after five seconds, but the sphere requires about five and a half seconds to become active again. Hit the sphere, wait about a second, then take the acceleration pad. If you time it right, the ceiling will rise just before you reach it, allowing you to grab the BFG and jump off before your enemy can trigger the switch and crush you.

Tip

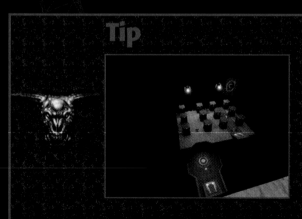

For a truly incredible vantage point, try rocket jumping off the high bounce pads. With a little air control, you can land on top of the crushing ceiling, making you immune from damage when it is triggered. If you have the railgun, you can score several kills before you can be easily targeted.

Quake III

The Capture The Flag Maps

Arena

DUELING KEEPS

WEAPONS: SHOTGUN, ROCKET LAUNCHER, RAILGUN, PLASMA GUN
POWER-UPS: NONE
POINT LIMIT: 8
RECOMMENDED TEAM SIZE: 3

1. The blue flag is on this platform.
2. Shotguns are here.
3. Yellow armor can be found in these locations.
4. Plasma guns are here.
5. Red armor is located in the fog area below this roof.
6. Rocket launchers are here.
7. The red flag can be found here.

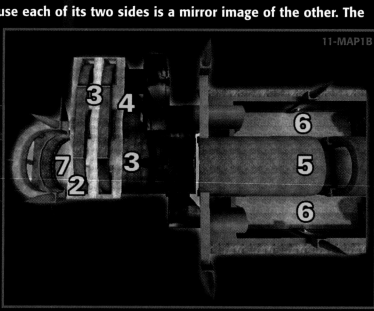

This map is interesting because each of its two sides is a mirror image of the other. The items are effectively in the same spot in each side, but each base is different. Starting from the flag in the blue base, you notice a pair of yellow healths behind the flag at the back of the rounded area. Off to the left is a shotgun, and to the right is a suit of yellow armor. A plasma gun sits on the floor beneath the yellow armor, and another suit of yellow armor rests in front of the pillar in the center of the room. You can exit via the bridge on the top of the map or the stairs from the yellow armor on the floor. Both paths lead to the middle area.

Tip

Although you can go through the door in the middle, doing so alerts your opponents that you are coming. A better and sneakier way is to jump through one of the windows on either side of the door.

The blue base holds enough weaponry and armor to make it defensible.

In the middle of the arena, there's a depression filled with fog. Staircases enter from both sides, but it's a short drop, easily made from either end. Red armor sits in this depression, and a rocket launcher lies at the top of the stairs on either side.

Heading into the red base, you find a mirror image of the blue base. There is a suit of yellow armor on the bridge on the right as you enter, and another one on the floor in front of the pillar. Again, the plasma gun sits on the

The doors between each base lead out to the central area, which is a frequent battle location.

bottom floor beneath the bridge, while the shotgun rests to the left of the flag. Just like the blue base, there is a pair of yellow healths behind the flag.

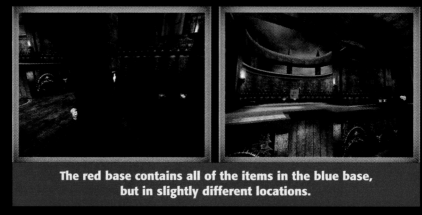

The red base contains all of the items in the blue base, but in slightly different locations.

TROUBLED WATERS

WEAPONS: SHOTGUN, GRENADE LAUNCHER, ROCKET LAUNCHER, RAILGUN, PLASMA GUN
POWER-UPS: MEGA-HEALTH, MEDKIT
POINT LIMIT: 8
RECOMMENDED
TEAM SIZE: 4-5

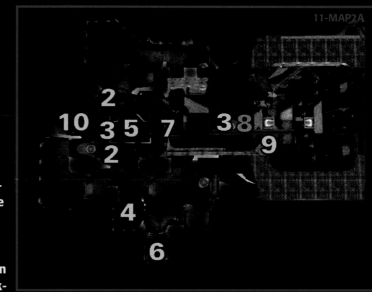

1. The red flag is on a shelf here.
2. There are grenade launchers in these four locations.
3. Suits of yellow armor are here.
4. Rocket launchers are situated in these small chambers.
5. Plasma guns are located in the middle of the two flag rooms.
6. Find Mega-Healths in these side chambers.
7. Railguns are located on these shelves overlooking the middle of the map.
8. Find shotguns here.
9. Medikits are located on each side of the central pool.
10. The blue flag is here.

There are several similar elements to the Brimstone Abbey map here. Both sides have bases that are set up in much the same way as the cathedral area in that map. The two bases and the paths to the center are identical. The flag is situated high on a shelf overlooking the cathedral area. There are two green healths situated just behind it. The only way up to the flag is via the angled bounce pad on the other side of the cathedral from the flag. Looking around the room, you see four distinct ways out. There are three doors on the ground floor, and at the back wall of each base there is a bounce pad leading to corridors behind the flag.

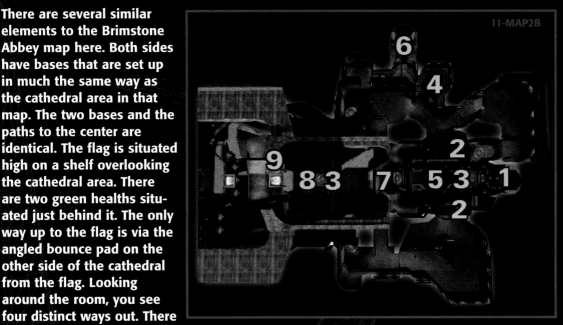

11-MAP2B

 Tip

The bounce pad to the flag can also be used to reach the ledges that look down on the flag. Like Brimstone Abbey, these shelves hold machine gun ammunition and gold health.

The bounce pad behind the flag takes you to a high corridor containing a grenade launcher and grenades. This corridor goes past a balcony that looks over the main floor of the base. This hall leads to two ways into the central area. The left branch enters onto the main floor while the right branch ends in a bounce pad that opens up to a balcony overlooking the central pool. This ledge extends all the way to the other side, leading into the opposite base.

If you've played through the deathmatch maps, this area should look very familiar.

Back in the base, on the ground floor, you can find both a suit of yellow armor and a plasma gun. A pair of yellow healths sits on the left side of the room. Directly in front of you, on either side of the bounce pad leading to the flag, there are doors leading out. There is also a third door on the right wall, near the yellow health.

Use this bounce pad to take you to a ledge overlooking the cathedral area, complete with a handy grenade launcher.

The first two doors both enter the same room. Enter the room and get the yellow armor near its center, then turn and look back in the direction of the flag. You can

see an alcove with a bounce pad inside. Jump here to reach a platform holding a railgun. This ledge overlooks the central courtyard, making it an excellent place to guard the base.

You can also take the bounce pad on the other side of the room. Or you can take the second bounce pad on the other side of the room. This heads up to the main floor of

The elevator leads up to a perfect spot to guard the main level of the map's center.

All roads lead to the middle eventually, even these two paths from the bounce pad in the cathedral area.

the central courtyard. A shotgun sits ahead and to the left. Also, directly in front of this entrance to the central courtyard is an acceleration pad that launches you over the pool in the middle of the room.

Back in the base, there is still the third door on the ground floor. Exit here and see the rocket launcher directly in front of you. The corridor turns to the left and up a set of stairs to a trio of armor shards and another door. A branching corridor

Use the bounce pad to reach the main floor of the arena's interior.

dead-ends at a Mega-Health. Go through the door and find a small, square room holding a shotgun and a pool of water.

Grab the medkit on your way through. As you come out of the tube into a small sunken chamber, immediately rise for air before entering the central pool. You have just enough air to make i t here without starting to drown. A ramp leads out of the water on each side.

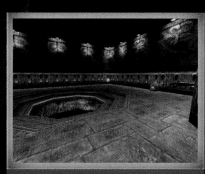

Up for a swim? This pool is another way into the enemy base.

Valuable items await in the basement.

Head up the stairs on either side, make an immediate right, and run past the yellow armor to the exit on the right side. If you turn right at the T-intersection, you discover a bounce pad that takes you up to a balcony running along one side of the central courtyard to the other base.

Grab the medkit in the twisting tunnel that leads to the outside.

Another balcony, another grenade launcher—perfect for your initial assault on the enemy flag.

Turn left at that intersection and run past a series of armor shards. This hallway ends in a second balcony that overlooks the main base area. Like the balcony on the other side, it is home to both a grenade launcher and a box of grenades.

This balcony is exposed, but it's not traveled as often as some of the other paths, making it somewhat safer. This is especially true if your enemies are asleep at the switch.

THE STRONGHOLD

WEAPONS: SHOTGUN, ROCKET LAUNCHER, RAILGUN, PLASMA GUN
POWER-UPS: QUAD, REGENERATION, INVISIBILITY
POINT LIMIT: 8
RECOMMENDED TEAM SIZE: 6

1. The blue flag is here.
2. Find the yellow armor here.
3. Regeneration icons are located on these platforms below the flags.
4. Shotguns are here.
5. You will find rocket launchers in these areas.
6. There is a cache of ammunition on each side of the level.
7. Find railguns here.
8. The central power-up can be found here.
9. The plasma gun spawns randomly in these four locations.
10. Find the red flag here.

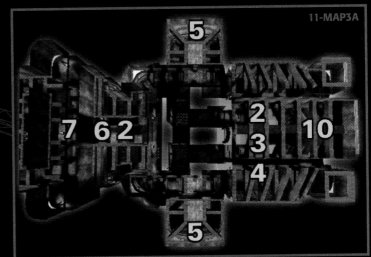

11-MAP3A

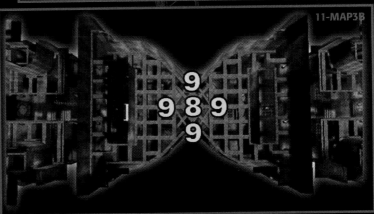

11-MAP3B

This map was designed specifically to be as challenging as possible for capture the flag players. Success on this map is tied heavily to working together as a team. For a player good with the railgun, the base can be held, since all three entrances are visible from the flag position. This makes it difficult to enter against a good team's base. At the same time, it is a difficult base to defend against a well-coordinated attack. Communication is the key to success on this map. The two sides are completely symmetrical.

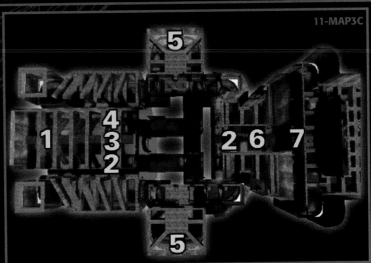

11-MAP3C

Starting at the flag, you can see three distinct ways into the base. Heading straight away from the flag , a staircase over the fog of death goes down to a landing. A regeneration icon appears in the middle of this landing, with yellow armor to the right and a shotgun to the left. There are two sets of stairs off this landing, one on each side, leading to the center of the map. These stairs go down to hallways that curve around the outside of the level, past a large cache of ammunition, and into the central area.

The flag area is difficult to defend against a well-organized attack, since enemies can come from the front or either side.

Both the right and left path along the top of the level from the flag take you past health and a box of rockets and railgun slugs. These halls also curve to the outside of the level. Like the lower floor, you can grab a string of armor shards here. Unlike the floor below, each path here also contains a rocket launcher.

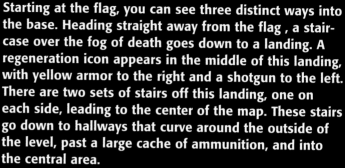

The top paths meet toward the center of the map at a suit of yellow armor, with a staircase leading away. Run down the stairs to find five green healths. A railgun sits at the end of the corridor here, and the corridor splits again, heading both right and left at the railgun. Each side leads to the central

There are four rocket launchers on this map, making it a popular weapon.

area. With the two entrances to the middle from the lower floor, there are four ways in from each base to the middle chamber, making it the site of many confusing and deadly melees.

Armor shards are available on both the top and bottom floor, but rocket launchers are available only on the top.

This ammo cache increases your firepower with virtually every weapon.

In the central chamber, the exact middle of the map is host to a power-up point. Five times out of seven, this holds a regeneration icon. The other two times, it holds a Quad or an invisibility icon, with an equal chance for either. The plasma gun also spawns in this central chamber at one of four points surrounding the central power-up.

Armor and health are always a good find, especially when leaving your side of the map or entering the enemy's.

The central area is often confusing because of the number of entrances.

As you can see, the two bases are identical.

The plasma gun appears in one of four spots around the central power-up.

SPACE CTF

WEAPONS: SHOTGUN, ROCKET LAUNCHER, RAILGUN, BFG10K
POWER-UPS: MEGA-HEALTH
POINT LIMIT: 8
RECOMMENDED
TEAM SIZE: 3-4

1. The blue flag is here.
2. Yellow armor is located in these four areas.
3. Rocket launchers are located here.
4. Find railguns on these high ledges.
5. The Mega-Health
   is here.
6. The BFG is located high above the map.
7. The red flag is here.

This level is unique in that it contains no ammunition except for the machine gun and the shotgun. The only way to increase your store of a particular type of ammunition is to find another weapon and pick it up. This level also takes place in outer space, making it just that much more deadly. This map is completely symmetrical.

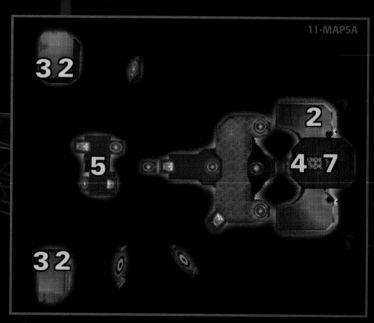

11-MAP5A

The flag sits on a platform at the back edge of the map. To the right of the flag is a suit of yellow armor, and to the left is a gold health. You can drop off the platform to a lower ledge, or make the riskier drop to a very low bounce pad.

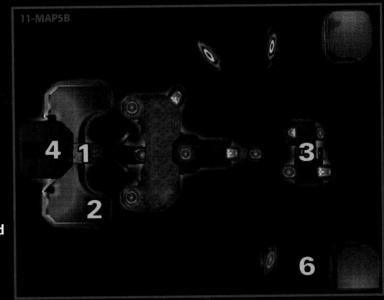

11-MAP5B

If you drop to the ledge, you find a very open platform containing only a gold health. Both of the bounce pads at the back of this platform take you back up to the flag. You can take the accelerator pad or drop to a third lower level. This level holds a bounce pad up to the middle floor and an acceleration pad that launches you across the map. Grab a rocket launcher on the way and land on the same level on the opposite side.

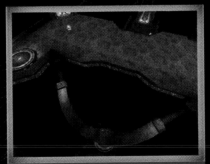

Now you have drops into the void to worry about in addition to your enemies.

Dropping to the ledge takes you on one trip, while heading for the bounce pad takes you on another.

The acceleration pad launches you through a pair of whirlpool-like openings that change your direction, firing you straight into the angled bounce pad in the middle of space. This pad launches you high into the air. You land on a high ledge overlooking the central platform of the map. There's a rocket launcher here, along with a suit of yellow armor. The only way off this platform, short of falling into space, is to drop down to the low platform at the center of the map.

This central platform holds a Mega-Health at its center. Each side of the platform holds both an angled bounce pad and an acceleration pad. Hit the bounce pad to launch yourself back to the level just under the flag. The acceleration pad takes you on a more interesting trip. It hurls you high into space onto a tiny platform

The Mega-Health is useful, but the position is exposed to everywhere on the map.

A high perch and a railgun make a perfect combination.

over the flag. This area contains a railgun, making it a perfect sniper's post.

The only unexplored path is the low bounce pad reachable both from the flag platform and the next level down. Bounce off this and rocket forward to a second bounce pad that takes you incredibly high over the central platform. If you control your jump slightly, you come down on a rocket launcher suspended over the Mega-Health.

There's a moving platform going back and forth high over the middle of the map. If

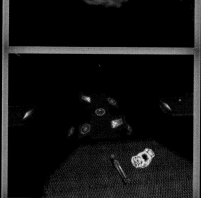

The whirlpools launch you forward into the bounce pads on the other end, which take you to the rocket launcher platform.

you can control your bounce off the second bounce pad, you can land on this. As it travels back and forth, it crosses just under a BFG10K, right where you can pick it up. Grab this, and you have a great perch from which to rain death on your opponents.

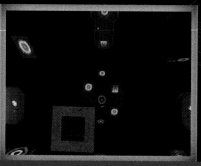

This bounce pad sends you high above the middle of the level.

If you can land on the moving platform, you can score the BFG.

Capture the Flag

There are some distinct differences between deathmatch games and team games. The most obvious distinction is that in a team game, not everyone is your enemy. There are other people that, rather than killing, you must work with to be successful. Nowhere is that more evident than in capture the flag.

The rules are simple. Although you can get personal points for fragging players on the other team, the only way to earn team points is by bringing the opposition's flag to your own home base. It sounds simple, but it's a little more complicated than that. To get a point, you must possess both flags in your base at the same time. So, if you grab the enemy flag and return it to your base, nothing happens unless you've also prevented the enemy team from taking your flag as well.

Naturally, the basic strategy in a game of this nature is to split your forces into two teams—an offensive team that attempts to steal the enemy flag and a defensive team that stays back at the base to protect your flag.

Both jobs are equally important. Without a good offense, you can't get the enemy flag. Without a good defense, you can't protect your own.

Protect your flag and take the enemy's. Everything else, even frags, is gravy in capture the flag.

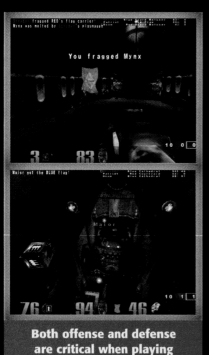

Both offense and defense are critical when playing capture the flag.

The most important aspect of capture the flag is cooperation. You must communicate with your teammates and know what the others are doing. If everyone decides to make a run on the flag, you have no one defending your base. If your teammate gets the flag and you aren't aware of it, you don't know to help him return successfully.

Constant communication with your team gives you a much greater chance of winning.

Defending your flag is a difficult job. You are guaranteed to see combat, and while you are more than likely acting from a protected area, you are not the one who initiates the combat in most cases. Therefore, you must be prepared for any eventuality.

Take a moment and explore the area around your flag. Look for all of the ways that an enemy might enter the area and reach your flag, particularly those ways that don't seem obvious at first. The back entrances are the ones your enemies will most likely take; few people march in through the front door. Examine the available weapons in the area and use what works best. When you are protecting confined spaces filled with walls and corners, area-effect weapons, like the rocket launcher, are your best choice. Large, open areas with good sight lines are perfect for defense with a railgun.

Look for bottleneck areas that your enemies are forced to come through. These are perfect places to defend. For example, in the first capture the flag map, enemies must enter your base through either the central door or the windows on either side. A position in this hallway allows you to see all of these entrances at once. Therefore, you can get off a shot or two at approaching enemies, weakening them while still giving you enough time to retreat to the flag to protect it.

Find and take as much armor in the area as you can. Not only does this better prepare you for the coming attack, but it also prevents incoming enemies from using that armor against you.

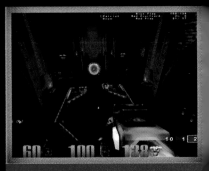

How many ways in are there to this area? How many different paths can an enemy take to get to your flag?

Bottlenecks like this one make great places to take a few initial shots at an enemy.

Keep moving. If you stand still, you're an easy target for an enemy moving in on your flag. Even if you are just doing a straight-line strafing movement, you are a harder target to hit if you keep moving. It's also easier to retaliate quickly if you are already moving and ready for battle than if you are standing still.

If the enemy gets your flag, pursue relentlessly. It does you no good to sit back in your base if there's no flag to guard. An enemy with the flag must be stopped, even if that means you get killed.

Even if you are just patrolling back and forth, you're more ready for battle if you keep moving.

Offense

Getting the enemy flag is an entirely different proposition than defending your own. When you defend, your desire is to draw your enemies into combat to keep the flag safe. If you can keep them away from the flag, or even delay them until help arrives, you've done your job. When you attack, the goal is to get in and out as quickly as possible.

When enemies have your flag, stop everything and hunt them down before they return to their base

Hit-and-run tactics are the way to go when trying to capture the enemy flag. Try to stay out of combat with the enemies guarding the flag. You have to throw some fire their way to clear them out of the area, but if you see an opening for the flag, take it. Don't get into gunfights because they give the other team's members time to retreat to their base and stop you.

Don't hang around the enemy base.
Get in and out as quickly as you can.

he most effective way to attack the enemy flag is to do so with a teammate. Operating essentially as wing-men for each other, you can dramatically increase the amount of firepower you can put on a single spot. Area-effect weapons are your best choice here, because they can clear out the area quickly, and not many peo-ple stand still during a barrage of rockets fired into their area.

Moving in with a teammate works well with hit-and-run tactics too. While one of you engages those guarding the flag, the other can run in and make a grab for it.

When you get the flag, run. Don't linger; don't try to find a better weapon. Don't even stop for health unless you desperately need it. Make a beeline for your goal and get the enemy flag there to score a point. Take the fastest route you can. A long, winding path back to your base really only means that there's more time for an enemy player to find and kill you.

Clear the area quickly, then take the flag and run.

You're always more powerful with a teammate.

If you have the flag, your job is to get back to your base as quickly as possible, not to score frags.

If your teammate gets the flag, your job becomes no less important. While he runs home for the point, you run inter-ference. Keep as many enemies off the player with the flag as possible. If you can get them to engage you in combat while your teammate runs clear, you've done your job. Do every-thing you can to keep the flag bearer safe, including moving in the way of enemy shots. Getting fragged is a small price to pay for your team scoring a point, and any hits that you take instead of the flag bearer make scoring more likely.

If it comes to it, be willing to die in defense of your flag, or in defense of your teammate with the enemy flag.

TEAMFRAG GAMES

Teamfrag games are about controlling areas of the arena which contain important assets (powerful weapons, armor and power ups) and using those assets to frag the opposition as much as possible. Your team scores points for every frag you score on the other team. However, killing one of your own team-mates reduces your score, as does accidentally killing yourself.

Area-effect weapons can be a little riskier in a team game.

This game combines elements of both capture the flag and deathmatch. Instead of protecting a flag, you decide which items in the arena are most important for success, such as the Quad or the rocket launcher. You then work to conquer or defend the areas containing those items so that your team controls them. Like with capture the flag, you are best off in most cases working with a teammate and concentrating your fire on one enemy at a time. This allows you to eliminate an enemy quickly before moving on to the next one. Having a partner also allows you to cover much more area at a time, since one of you can concentrate on one side of a room while the other scans the opposite side.

A trickier element of teamfrag is dividing up the items you come across. It goes without saying that the player who is more badly wounded should get the health when you find it. But how do you decide who gets which weapon? For starters, you can clear up some of these questions before the match begins. If you are good with, or simply prefer, a particular weapon, let your teammates know.

Teamwork counts in team games. You not only score more frags, you draw less fire.

If both of you want a given weapon, have one of you take it, then wait for the respawn. The two of you will then have to guard the room or area for the 30 seconds needed for the weapon to reappear. As with capture the flag games, cooperation and communication are the keys to being successful.

Who gets the health? It depends on who needs it more.

Another aspect of communication is keeping your teammates informed of important events. If you notice that enemies are camping in a particular location, tell your teammates. You can either plan a way to attack and knock them out of the area, or simply warn the others of the possible ambush.

There are, of course, aspects of teamfrag that are similar to deathmatch. Go for the weaker players on

Communication with your teammates is critical.

If you already have a weapon and your teammate doesn't, give it up. The better armed your team as a whole is, the better chance you have of winning.

the enemy team whenever possible, and continually listen for the sound of an enemy player spawning in after a death. The faster your side can rack up frags, the faster you win. Along the same lines, do what you can to protect the weakest player on your team from the enemy. While you shouldn't necessarily have to nursemaid anyone, take some extra precautions, such as allowing your teammate to grab additional health or armor, or even a more powerful weapon to defend with.

As with any deathmatch game, going for the weaker enemies pays off with a higher number of frags.

It's important to remember that in teamfrag, you win and lose as a team. It's great to be the highest-scoring member of your team, but if you lose, it doesn't really mean much. Therefore, don't get too upset if another member of your team comes in and "steals" a frag from you by killing an enemy you were dueling with. After all, a frag is a frag, and each one helps your team, regardless of how you get it.

Don't be afraid to retreat in a teamfrag game, especially just after you respawn in after dying. You don't have to take on the enemy by yourself, and if you are only armed with your machine gun, there's probably others on your team better equipped to handle an enemy than you are. Let them do it, since attacking foolishly doesn't just get you killed, it gives the other team a frag. After spawning in, try to find a few useful items before you run back into battle. Let your teammates handle the enemy until you are strong enough to join in. They'll be happy you did, since this will keep you from getting killed and adding to the enemy team's score.

Any frag for your team is a good frag, even if you aren't the one who scores it.

After you respawn, find items quickly. Let your teammates handle the fight until you are strong enough to join in.

I3uAKE

Advanced Quake III Arena Tactics

ARENA

Improving Your Fighting Skills

You can rocket jump up to excellent sniping positions. You can use a railgun without shooting yourself in the foot. But you just don't seem to score enough frags to be taken seriously by the great players out there. What do you do? Practice, certainly. Fighting well is a combination of both skill and brains. Not only do you have to know how to use a railgun, you must also know when to use it, the best places to use it, and when you shouldn't use it. The following ideas will help both your physical and mental skills to make you a truly top-notch deathmatch, capture the flag, or team deathmatch player.

In normal situations, you use the mouse much like you use your head. Your movements tend to be regular instead of jerky.

The Mouse Flick

You're running down a corridor, when suddenly you start taking damage. Since there's no one in front of you, your attacker must be to your rear. What do you do, stop and turn? Of course not—this would make you an easy target. The solution is the "mouse flick," a trick that requires some practice to perfect, but once learned, can save you from a lot of danger.

When playing, you tend to use the mouse much as you

Switching from running forward to running backward is essential for this maneuver. It allows you to continue moving in the same direction while returning fire.

would your head, to look around. While your movements aren't slow with the mouse, they tend to be regular. The mouse flick requires that you do something else with the mouse. A fast flick against the desktop spins you rather than simply turning you, and you pirouette between steps. Practice this move until you can consistently spin 180 degrees.

The second part of the mouse flick is to switch from running forward to running backward as you do the flick. Now, you're still headed in the same direction as you were before, but you're facing the opposite direction, right at your enemy. Then to complete the maneuver, start firing. This way, someone coming up behind you gets instant retaliation.

Practice this move and use it frequently, and not just in combat. Use it to grab items out of alcoves or near edges and corners. You have a clear view of the area around you, still get the item, and take fewer shots in the back. This does take practice, but the practice pays off.

Learn to back onto items instead of facing walls and corners so you can continue to scan your environment.

WHO TO KILL

Predators in the wild don't kill the healthy animals. They kill the very old, the very young, the lame, and the sick. Why? Because they are easier prey. This is a perfect lesson for you. Your prey in *Quake III Arena* should be the weakest in the bunch. Find the weakest player, or the player in the worst position, and move in for the kill.

A part of you might be saying that this hardly seems fair, and that may be true. It is, however, a reality. In a deathmatch situation, it makes sense to go for the weakest opponent because that's the best way to increase your number of frags. Naturally, you shouldn't avoid battle with anyone else, or run from a fight if someone else targets you. Just attempt to engage the weakest player whenever you can.

Concentrate on the weakest player, human or computer-controlled.

Should you pass up a healthy opponent just to get to a weaker one? Not necessarily, but try to engage the weaker opponent when you can.

Along those same lines, listen for the sound of people spawning in after dying. A character, when freshly spawned, is armed only with a machinegun and the gauntlet, while you probably have much more powerful weapons. A newly spawned character is a much easier kill than one who has been active for some time, even a wounded one. While sportsmanship certainly has its place, every active opponent can frag you, so frag them when you have the advantage.

Characters spawning in have no armor and little weaponry, making them perfect targets.

Tip

Concerned about the fairness of attacking the weakest player or characters spawning in? Remember, they would do the same to you.

Brains Versus Brawn

Some people say that thinking has very little place in a game like *Quake III*. Those people are wrong. Skill is incredibly important, but it's not always what matters when playing against other human opponents. This is true in one-on-one competition, as well as wild group deathmatches. The best players use skill and brains to be successful.

In spite of what the action junkies might tell you, there is plenty of room in the game for thinking and going about things logically. This isn't always easy in a frenzied deathmatch against six other people, but it is essential for success. Brainpower has its place in the single-player game as well. Since you are the only combatant in the single player game in the Arena Eternal with a human brain, you're the only one capable of outthinking your enemies.

Skill is important, but not as important as brain power.

ARMOR AND HEALTH

It is very important to keep yourself protected. However, it's easy to be either too conservative or too liberal in terms of armor and health. Naturally, it's better to have more health and armor than less. But when do you go for armor, and when do you go for health?

Really, it all depends on the situation. If you are in combat, don't make a run for health or armor unless you can get it without turning your back on your enemy, unless you are desperate.

Between battles, go for armor and health, especially armor. You can always use any armor you can find, and grabbing it prevents your opponents from getting it. If you are simply moving from place to place, get any health you pass by as well. There's not a huge difference between 97 health and 100 health, but there is a difference. More than one frag has been scored by a player with a single point of health. However, if you are moving from one place to another with a specific purpose in mind (like getting the Quad), don't sidetrack for health unless you are badly wounded.

If you can grab armor or health in combat, good. If you have to break off combat to heal, make sure you really need it. Otherwise, keep fighting.

Tip

Remember, denying things to your opponents keeps them weak and helps you kill them more easily.

There's a time to fight and a time to back off. Don't run away just because of a little damage.

Don't become obsessive about armor and health. There's a lot more to do than simply run from room to room looking for health and suits of yellow armor. You'll never score a frag if you're so concerned about maintaining your health that you retreat at the first sign of damage.

Don't be scared to do something that might hurt you. Taking a long fall is only dangerous if you have just a few points of health left, and it can save you a lot of time getting from place to place. The same is true with rocket or BFG jumping. It's not natural to do something that hurts you. However, if there's health and armor nearby to replace what you've lost, and you can save a lot of time by doing so, you are remiss to avoid a weapon jump just because it takes away a few points of health.

Don't be afraid to rocket jump or take a long fall if it helps you in the long run.

Grabbing Weapons and Ammunition

It's important to remember that weapons spawn after about five seconds, and armor, health, and ammunition take about 30 seconds to reappear. Therefore, don't be afraid to use a weapon with only a few shots left. Even if someone else picks up the weapon as it spawns in, a new one will replace it in just a few seconds.

And speaking of weapons, there is a right way and a wrong way to pick them up, especially for the first time on a level or after a respawn. It's a subtle difference, but it's an important difference to understand.

Each weapon has a default amount of ammunition: 10 shots for the shotgun, grenade launcher, rocket launcher, and railgun, 20 for the BFG10K, 50 for the plasma gun, and 100 for the lightning gun. Picking up a spawned weapon for the first time gives you the default amount. Therefore, if you pick up a spawned rocket launcher without already having one, you get 10 rockets with it. If you already have some ammunition for that weapon, picking up a spawned weapon still only gives you the default amount. Therefore, if you pick up a box of rockets, which holds five rockets, then pick up your first rocket launcher, you still only have ten rockets, the default amount. Furthermore, if you already have the default amount (or more) of ammunition for a weapon, you only get a single round, shot, or rocket. Naturally, this means you should grab the weapon before you grab the ammunition boxes.

Grabbing a new weapon should be done with some thought to the situation and the other weapons available.

There is a right way to pick up weapons to get the maximum amount of ammunition. In emergency or combat situations, don't worry about it. Just fight, and think about picking up weapons when the battle is over.

Switch weapons when you have to. Rocket launchers and railguns are bad at close range, and shotguns aren't that great from halfway across the map.

It gets a little bit more complicated when you factor in dropped weapons. An enemy holding a rocket launcher drops it when killed. When you pick this up, it adds the default amount to your total. So, if you already have a rocket launcher with 10 rockets, and you pick up a dropped rocket launcher, you'll have 20 rockets—your original 10, plus the default amount added to your total for picking up the dropped weapon.

In short, grab the spawned weapons first, then go for dropped weapons and ammunition boxes. This increases your supply of ammunition, which is important in the middle of a battle. Nothing is worse than running out of shotgun shells or plasma cells right when you're about to frag an enemy.

Which rocket launcher should you grab? Well, if you already have one, get the spawned rocket launcher in front of you before you get the dropped one behind it.

This brings up another important point. Switching weapons in battle is recommended only when doing so greatly increases your chances of success. Changing weapons takes time, perhaps not much, but even a second can be too long. Switch when you need to switch, but otherwise, stick with the weapon you've got.

Tip

Turn off the automatic weapon switching option on your player setup. Running across a weapon while in combat with this option on automatically switches you to the new weapon, which can cost you some critical seconds.

The Psychological War

Keeping control of the battle is more than simply fragging as fast as you can, especially in a one-on-one situation. Against a human opponent, there are many things you can do to take control of a battle. Frags are important, but so is controlling the tempo of the battle.

In short, you want to be the one who determines when to fight and when not to fight. You want battles to be fought on your terms, not on your opponent's terms. If you can dictate when combat occurs, you have a significant advantage. You know when you have to be cautious; your opponent does not. You know when combat will happen while your opponent expects it at any time.

You have to fight sometime, but you'll fare better if you are the one who decides when to fight and when not to.

Study the maps, particularly the final map for each of the tiers, since these are the ones most likely used for one-on-one play. Look at them from a strategic perspective. Take the tournament map from the second tier (The Proving Grounds) as an example. You can cover the central area containing the rocket launcher from the top level while still guarding against an opponent attacking from either side. There's no need to actually patrol that basement area, other than getting the rocket launcher, since you can do it more effectively from another location.

Find positions that allow you to cover a lot of territory at once.

Perhaps the most important aspect of game domination is the denial of items to enemies. Learn the maps. Learn where all of the items are, and learn how long it takes you to get from place to place. If you can create a patrol area that allows you to keep particular items out of the hands of your enemies, you've earned a serious psychological victory. Concentrate on a single item at first, and as you become more and more adept at keeping it away from your enemy, expand your ability to incorporate more items. Knowing the time it takes to move around the map is critical. If it takes 15 seconds to move between two items, you have time to get one, move to the other, and return to the first just as it respawns.

Keeping an item out of an enemy's hands keeps you more powerful, and frustrates your opponent.

Tip

It's best to use this strategy with items like armor. Since weapons respawn every five seconds, it is almost impossible to keep them out of enemy hands.

Note

As you learn the maps and start to employ this strategy, expect to lose. As you improve, though, you'll start to develop a feel for what your opponent is doing, and you'll be able to deny him particular items whenever you wish, thanks to your practice.

It's best to concentrate on learning one map at a time, but don't let this dissuade you from playing on other maps as well. Seeing other maps, and what other players do on them, can give you some new ideas for the map that you are concentrating on.

Keep an awareness of the map as a whole rather than just concentrating on yourself and your opponent or opponents. Try to be aware of the items that have been picked up and when they will spawn back in. Know where the more powerful areas of a level are and where the places are that are difficult to defend. Combine this with your ability to deny items to opponents, and keep them mired in the less-powerful areas of the map.

As you are learning a map, pay attention to everything around you. Apply what you have learned from other arenas to your chosen one.

When will the items that appear here respawn? You need to know if you want to succeed.

Tip

Try to imagine the battle from the other player's perspective. Then do what you would least like to see your opponent do if you were in his position.

These ideas are difficult to put into practice, but they do work. And don't underestimate the psychological advantage this gives you over a human opponent. Denying items, or entire areas of the map, to your enemies makes them feel helpless. It also gives you a very real advantage in terms of items and possibly weaponry, and allows you to control the initiative of the battle and the flow of the combat. Take any advantage you can get and keep it. Never give up a physical or psychological advantage on an opponent. If you can undermine your enemies' confidence, you'll find them easier to frag.

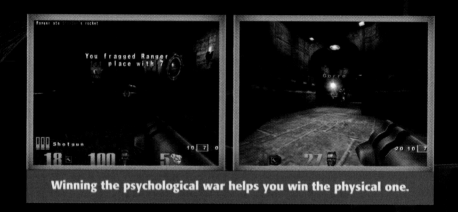

Winning the psychological war helps you win the physical one.

Finally, talk to other players, especially those who beat you. Ask them what they do and how you can improve. Some players won't help you, but others will. The best players want their competition to get better, since it helps them improve their own game. Watch what other players do. Enter games as a spectator and observe the tactics used by the best players.

14

QUAKE

Skin Creation and New Levels

ARENA

Creating Skins and New Levels

After playing *Quake III Arena* for some time, you may find the desire to create your own personalized skin. Whether because you are tired of the skins that are available in the game or want to express your own creativity, the creation of a skin for *Quake III Arena* is an excellent way to become more involved with the *Quake* community. You can also do this by creating your own levels for play.

The following online resources can get you started in creating your own skins, contain useful FAQs about skin creation and level creation, or contain a number of skins and levels you can download to use in *Quake III Arena*.

Site Name	URL
3Dpalette	http://3dpalette.com/
666 Skins	http://www.quake2.com/skins/
The Bin	http://www.geocities.com/TimesSquare/Arcade/5610/thebin/
Blue's News	http://www.bluesnews.com/
Freetextures	http://www.freetextures.com/freetextures.html
GENSurf	http://planetquake.com/gensurf/
The NecroHunter's Lair	http://www.3dpalette.com/necrohunter/
Nevication Graphics	http://www.3dpalette.com/nevication/
Pandemonium	http://www.planetquake.com/pandemonium/
Planet Quake	http://www.planetquake.com/
Polycount	http://www.planetquake.com/polycount/
Q-Workshop 3	http://qw3.telefragged.com/
Q3Center	http://www.q3center.com/
QERadiant	http://www.qeradiant.com/

Site Name	URL
Q U A D Artistic Authority	http://www.planetquake.com/quad/
Quake 3 Arena Skins	http://q3skins.homepage.com/
Quake 3 World	http://www.quake3world.com/
Quake Gallery	http://www.planetquake.com/qgallery/
Rorschach's Journal	http://www.quakefiles.com/rorshach
RUST	http://www.gamedesign.net/
Scary's Shuga Shack	http://www.shugashack.com/
Shattered Art	http://www.planetquake.com/shattered/
Sheol's Web	http://www.cix.co.uk/~nanzinjal/
The Skin Factory	http://www.planetquake.com/factory/
The Skinforge	http://www.planetquake.com/skinforge/
Skin-Tech	http://skintech.vekoduck.com/
Skin Workshop	http://skin-workshop.quake2.co.uk/
Skinning 101	http://squadron.telefragged.com/skin101/
Skinsurgeon	http://www.clanworld.dk/skinsurgeon/
Skins Tutorial	http://www.planetquake.com/skintutor/frames.html
SKUN	http://www.q3center.com/skun/
STOMPED	http://www.stomped.com/
StrangeFate's Skins Page	http://www.planetquake.com/strangefate

Quake III Arena™
T-Shirts, Hats & Mousepads!

L, XL
$14.99
+ S & H*

$9.99
+ S & H*

$14.99
+ S & H*

Order Yours Today at www.activision.com

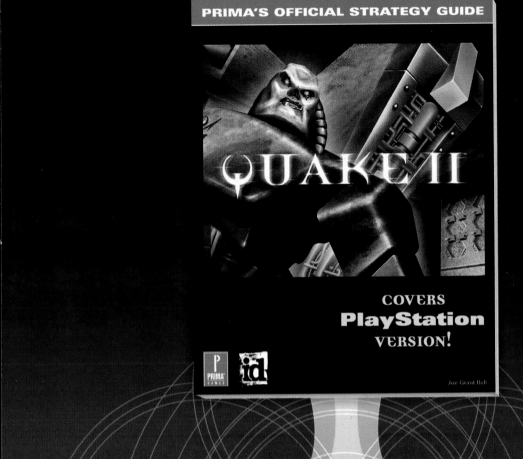

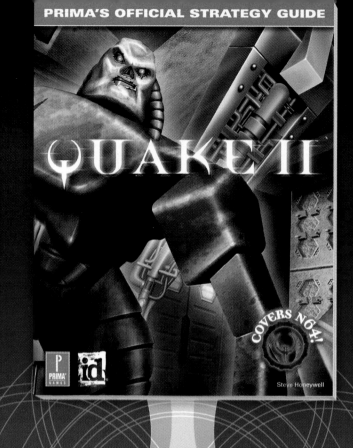